the TERRIBLE PARADOX *of* SELF-AWARENESS

Also by Robert Pantano

The Art of Living an Absurd Existence
The Closer We Get
Millions of Little Threads
The Art of Living a Meaningless Existence
The Hidden Story of Every Person
Notes from the End of Everything

the TERRIBLE PARADOX *of* SELF-AWARENESS

how awareness is the
beginning and end of suffering

ROBERT PANTANO

Andrews McMeel
PUBLISHING®

The authorised representative in the EEA is Simon and Schuster Netherlands BV, Herculesplein 96 3584 AA Utrecht, Netherlands. (info@simonandschuster.nl)

Andrews McMeel Publishing
a division of Andrews McMeel Universal
1130 Walnut Street, Kansas City, Missouri 64106

www.andrewsmcmeel.com

26 27 28 29 30 TEN 10 9 8 7 6 5 4 3 2 1

ISBN: 979-8-8816-0234-5

Library of Congress Control Number: 2025945558

Cover source images licensed under Pixabay and CC0 1.0
Cover collage by Robert Pantano

Editor: Melissa R. Zahorsky
Art Director: Tiffany Meairs
Production Editor: Kayla Overbey
Production Manager: Julie Skalla

Contents

Introduction

At some point in history, a human asked the first question, striking the flint of comprehension against the pyrite of uncertainty. In that moment, the first true spark of humanity's self-awareness was produced—a spark destined to light the world on fire.

Self-awareness is generally considered a good thing. As a result of our unique human form of self-awareness, we can conceptually comprehend ourselves and the world, abstractly recall and foresee events, form rationales about the things that happen, and strive to change them. These abilities are undeniably profound. They have played a fundamental role in our rising to the top of the animal kingdom, overcoming the inhibitions of our biology, and conquering much of the world. But self-awareness can also be a terrible thing. Because of our particular form of it, we can also realize our own limits; we can perceive, with grave intensity, our ignorance, meekness, futility, and suffering.

As individuals capable of comprehending, imagining, and rationalizing, we are naturally compelled toward understanding, controlling, and mattering. The problems caused by our self-awareness begin here, with the contrast between what we are compelled toward and what we are capable of. Although we are granted the ability to comprehend some of ourselves and reality, and although we can conquer so much of the world, ultimately, we do not seem to possess the ability to truly control, understand, or conquer ourselves. As a species, we don't really know what we want. Human progress, both individually and collectively, is often passionate but also largely blind and aimless, all roads apparently leading toward futility and oblivion.

Even if we knew what we wanted, all evidence seems to suggest that we would only struggle indefinitely to attain it. We can never quite dig deeply enough into ourselves and the world to know what's at play—to know what mechanisms of nature are in operation, why they work the way they do, and how or whether we can fundamentally alter how they work.

We will never obtain what we are truly after. We can never conquer reality and know truth. Every new discovery will inevitably fall victim to the next. Every attempt at meaning will inevitably reveal itself to be an illusion. The more tightly we try to hold on to the world, the more our hands will callous. Ultimately, we all must watch ourselves as we struggle against these inevitabilities; we must witness our failures, our absurdities, and our deaths as we strive endlessly—with a reasonably clear view but no clear direction. It is as if we are given access to the show of existence with the desire for a directorial role, but, with intense lucidity, we are forced to sit in the audience as things go wrong over and over. The cultural anthropologist Ernest Becker brilliantly summarizes our existential plight in *The Denial of Death:*

> Man has a symbolic identity that brings him sharply out of nature. He is a symbolic self, a creature with a name, a life history. He is a creator with a mind that soars out to speculate about atoms and infinity. . . .
>
> Yet, at the same time . . . man is a worm and food for worms. This is the paradox: he is out of nature and hopelessly in it; he is dual, up in the stars and yet housed in a heart-pumping, breath-gasping body that once belonged to a fish and still carries the gill-marks to prove it. . . . It is a terrifying dilemma to be in and to have to live with.

Of course, the problems of self-awareness are by no means new. They began at the onset of consciousness, and then, arguably, they became more and more inflamed throughout human history—through the cognitive revolution, agricultural revolution, scientific revolution, industrial revolutions, and technological revolutions. But now, particularly because of the rapid progress of science and technology, we are suddenly more aware of ourselves and the world than any humans have ever been before. We are more aware of the horrors and paradoxes of our existence. Moreover, because of the modernization and Westernization of so much of the world, we are also more compelled to understand, control, and eradicate these horrors and paradoxes. Western society has largely chosen reason, order, control, and certainty as its weapons in the war against the universe. But every battle is fought in a war that cannot be won. The universe feels no pain. We feel the pain for it. The war is thus with ourselves. We have been and will always be the victims of our own tactics.

Over time, though we have increasingly prospered in areas like safety, security, health, and longevity, we have, arguably, declined in areas like our sense of meaning, purpose, connection, and clarity. Previous myths and imagined orders that depended on humanity's ignorance have fallen increasingly to the wayside, killed off by new knowledge and theories. Folklores, mythologies, religions, traditions—these things have been sacrificed to our increasing awareness. In the words of the author H. P. Lovecraft:

> The most merciful thing in the world, I think, is the inability of the human mind to correlate all its contents. We live on

> a placid island of ignorance in the midst of black seas of infinity, and it was not meant that we should voyage far. The sciences, each straining in its own direction, have hitherto harmed us little; but some day the piecing together of dissociated knowledge will open up such terrifying vistas of reality, and of our frightful position therein, that we shall either go mad from the revelation or flee from the deadly light into the peace and safety of a new dark age.

The "some day" that Lovecraft wrote about nearly one hundred years ago is, arguably, *today.* The human project appears to be one lifelong response to having woken up to these "terrifying vistas"—the conditions of reality and consciousness—and then trying to outrun them by running further into them. And now, we have fully opened them up. And they cannot be escaped. Thus, confronting the pains and problems of self-awareness has only become increasingly crucial.

It is not hopeless. Although our self-awareness causes much of our suffering, it is also the lifeline with which we can manage and endure it. Self-awareness is the means by which we can transmute and transcend our suffering. More crucially and powerfully than anything else, because of our awareness, we are uniquely able to discover and interpret immense beauty and wonder—despite what we cannot do or know, and despite how terrifying everything might be. Not only are we able to exist and survive, but we can exist and survive in the name of ideas and wonders that we forge for ourselves. With proper attention and effort, we can weave meaning out of our bodies, our minds, our nature, our history, and our future, like a tapestry of possibility and achievement. We can know ourselves and know that we know ourselves. We can know the borders of knowledge and struggle against them, pushing like a child might against a heavy piece of furniture that they have no business moving—but if it even moves an inch, joy floods the veins. We can transfigure suffering into meaning—through art, curiosity, and aesthetic experiences. We can know why it means so much to draw close to another being. We can know what it means to love—and we can choose to love it all. This is the terrible paradox of self-awareness: Our awareness causes our suffering, but our suffering can be made worthwhile through our awareness. The task is not to resolve this paradox, however, but to utilize and embrace it.

on the problem of self-awareness

He knows so much and yet so little.

He sees the world through a pinhole chiseled out by his consciousness, forging a view of the chaos out from the blackened nothingness of eternity.

He is scared, confused, and alone.

There is no greater disorientation than waking up with the capacity to perceive, think, and comprehend while having no idea why or for what.

◆

No one knows their origin story. No one knows their purpose.

◆

Prior to humanity's development of self-awareness, life had only played the game of survival. Following the development of self-awareness, life began to also play the game of meaning. Existence was no longer a matter of *being,* but a matter of *being something for a reason.* So it began: an endless charade of impossibility.

◆

To be born into consciousness is to be pulled away from the *true reality* of things. It is to emerge from *nothingness* into a distorted permutation of *everything,* invariably filtered by and contained inside one's mind. It is to suddenly believe in and cling to being separate from everything else; it is to suddenly believe in *everything else;* it is to see a reality as a plurality of individual objects and phenomena; it is to create and know chaos.

◆

To live as a conscious being is to strive endlessly toward reobtaining the fundamental nature of reality—the bliss of nothingness.

◆

Every being is a non-consenting participant in existence—a victim to themselves and the will of nature that conceived them. We are all unavoidably coerced into thinking and wanting and believing.

◆

The human brain is wired to yearn for the continuation of itself, to attach itself to the idea of itself, and to defend itself unyieldingly. All this, and yet the only apparently clear fact of its nature is that it must decay and end. Worse, it must know of this the whole time.

In that moment somewhere just after our birth, when we first stepped into our unique image of the world, we were set up to lose often and significantly. We were positioned against the imperative of consciousness to desire comfort, control, certainty, and continuance, while simultaneously positioned against the imperative of the world that prohibits consciousness from any of these things. Consciousness must be the most absurd condition! It is fundamentally compelled toward what it cannot and will not ever obtain.

◆

We never had a choice. We never had a chance.

◆

It is only through being born that one is faced with the certainty of death. It is only through consciousness that one is faced with the awareness of this certainty. And it is through this awareness that the absurdity of humankind's condition is born.

◆

At the inception of humanity's unique form of consciousness, it began weaving a web that it would inevitably catch itself in, becoming both the spider and the fly, perpetuating the suffering of itself through its continual desire, creation, and consumption, forced to watch itself struggle in its own mouth.

◆

It is, at times, easy to be envious of those in the earliest stages of human history—humans who had the ability to know, but did not yet know, or better yet, did not care to know, about the nature and implications of existence. Their concerns were likely found in the eyes of lions and storms, not in the eyes of black holes and the oblivion of all things.

◆

The worst calamities of humankind, individual and collective, are not the fault of any single person, group, civilization, or state. They are the fault of consciousness—its delusive self-belief and sense of righteousness.

◆

Our consciousness was the greatest accident.

◆

We know just enough to know that we know basically nothing. We long to know the answers—why we must live and die and feel the pains of it all—only to live and die without reason, never having touched anything close to an answer.

◆

We can never know when and how the first question was asked, but we can know that following this moment, we have forever thereafter found ourselves captured by our own mind on a journey down and through a seemingly unending rabbit hole of question and answer, question and answer, question and uncertainty.

Self-awareness has sent us on a journey of impossibility.

◆

Human existence is sandwiched between unknowns—before and after; inside and outside.

◆

Once born into this existence, we are forever trapped within it as ourselves, only capable of knowing what we can perceive and comprehend during this time and stage of our existence. Everything else is unknown and unknowable.

◆

There is no escaping one's existence—not through death, not through immortality. One's existence is and will forever be contained within oneself.

◆

To be conscious is to believe in and attach to a self only for it to ultimately dissolve away forever like a mirage that disappears when the light changes; it is to fall in love with the things around you; it is to know of love and beauty and possibility while simultaneously knowing that hidden within them is the pain, tragedy, and loss of all things. Consciousness is a cruelty of evolution.

◆

We are perhaps the only beings who not only feel the possibility of things going wrong, but also *know,* as a matter of fact, that things will go wrong.

◆

In each car horn or lost set of keys, in each quarrel with a colleague or romantic partner, in each moment of quiet frustration or discomfort, hunger or cramps, we are reminded of our ignorant, helpless primality—that we are both animal and man, caught in the broken gears of consciousnesses, trying to grapple with the nature of a beast, the mind of a god, and a universe of desolation.

◆

With every beat, our hearts seem to pound on the locked door of the chest, pleading to escape the inescapable.

◆

It is often suggested that one should be grateful to be alive. We *are* in a miraculously unlikely position—to be alive and conscious. Shouldn't we be grateful for what is so unlikely? Not if what is so unlikely is also so unfortunate.

It isn't clear whether to be conscious is fortunate or unfortunate. Ask me in one moment, and I'll spell out my gratitude and wonder with the most intense poeticism I can possibly muster. Ask me a day or even an hour later, and I'll deny it with the same fervor.

◆

Self-awareness is a sort of poison that we each consume upon birth. Our choice invariably becomes the following: to relinquish our consciousness or to learn to blend it into an elixir. The latter takes the intelligence of a chemist and the magic of a sorcerer. Perhaps self-awareness, somehow, provides us with the poison, intelligence, and magic all at once.

◆

Determining whether life is worth living, in the words of the philosopher Albert Camus, "amounts to answering the fundamental question of philosophy." But there is a more fundamental question, as this question of whether life is worth living necessitates a prior question. *Is consciousness positive or negative?* Consciousness makes the *fundamental problem of philosophy* possible. A plant or dog does not care if life is worth living. They just live. Life need not be worth living to a living being for which this question never arises. Only to the conscious human does this question arise, and so only through consciousness is such a problem possible. Thus, deciding *whether consciousness is a good or bad thing* is to answer the fundamental question of philosophy.

◆

Humanity cannot renounce its consciousness, because humanity *is* its consciousness. So humanity must either renounce itself or learn how to live well with its consciousness—to love its consciousness. This is the task of philosophy in the broadest sense: to find wisdom and live well.

on the nature of consciousness

He does not understand and can never understand why he understands anything. He does not know why the dead matter that makes up one part of his body lets him think and feel while the same matter of another part does not. His consciousness is beyond his consciousness.

He cannot comprehend himself, and the world cannot comprehend him. He is alone in his head, hidden from the world within the greatest mystery no one can ever solve.

Everything that constitutes one's being is completely dead. Yet somehow, when put together in such a way, it lives. More significantly, it becomes aware.

Unlike seemingly all other arrangements of matter in the universe, the human brain can know of *itself;* it can know that it *is* matter; and it can know that its unique arrangement of matter, unlike other arrangements, can know these things.

How do the electrical signals of otherwise lifeless matter equate to conceptual understanding? How do they equate to the experiences of wonder, pain, happiness, sadness, color, sweetness, sharpness, and everything else? How do they allow us to imagine objects and places that don't otherwise exist?

Imagine an empty parking lot at night. What is this parking lot? Where is it? How does it exist inside one's mind without any source for it beyond the unrelated, detached matter and electrical impulses of the brain? There is no source for this parking lot other than *memories.* But memories are nothing more than clusters of brain cells. These cells are not a parking lot. They contain nothing *like a parking lot.* And yet there in one's mind is a parking lot. Even more confounding, there is no central point in the mind for the *image* or *experience* of this parking lot to be displayed. We know there is an experience of an idea or perhaps image of a parking lot somewhere in our mind, but where in our *mind?* Who or what is displaying this imagined scene, and who or what is viewing it? It feels like there is a stage or screen where thoughts and objects of our imagination are shown to us. It feels like there is an *us.* But there is not. There is no central place. There is no distinct *us.* There is no clear delineation between thought and thinker. It is all one constant process, everything happening all at once.

◆

The experiences of being something and being aware of that something seemingly just appear out of nothingness—not only from nothingness into existence but from matter into consciousness.

◆

If a rock suddenly articulated itself, we would all perceive this as some sort of miracle, and we would not believe our eyes and ears. And yet in every moment in which we *know* we have eyes and ears—able to see, hear, and know at all—we exhibit the same sort of miracle—the same apparently lifeless matter of the universe becoming conscious, knowing itself. In the words of the philosopher Douglas Harding in *On Having No Head:*

> Raise your little finger, blink an eyelid, notice the hospitality you're according to these printed shapes and those sounds—the vividness they owe to the depth and clarity of the room you give them—and admit you have no idea how you perform these and a million other miracles.

◆

Perhaps consciousness is merely the output of the information processing in the brain. Perhaps it isn't even really *doing* anything. It is, rather, merely an emergent phenomenon caused by the highly complex arrangement of matter in the human brain. It is a result rather than a feature.

Consider how the screen on a phone, TV, or computer is not involved in the mechanics of the device, but rather, it simply displays what the mechanics of the device do. Perhaps consciousness is the *screen* to the brain. But since *we* are our consciousness, unlike in the case of these technological devices, our sense of self-awareness, or our sense of interfacing with our brain, is not separate from and does not affect what the brain does. We are not controlling the screen. We *are* the screen. To make this clearer, imagine if while you were watching something on a device, the screen, and only the screen, stopped working and lighting up. The inner mechanics of the device would still work fine. One would just no longer be able to see the display of the device's mechanics. Likewise, perhaps with exception to displaying the functions of the brain, consciousness is entirely unneeded to the functions of the brain. But, of course, at the functional level and complexity of the human brain, the screen is always lit.

◆

Consciousness is a phenomenon created by nature. It is a product of evolution. Evolution is the process by which the traits and biological phenomena that enhance the likelihood of survival are passed on and sustained by successive generations of a population and species. Consciousness is thus not created *for* the individual who experiences it. It is, in fact, largely created without regard for our individual, subjective experience of it. Only insofar as the quality of our subjective experience promotes survival and reproduction is such quality likely to have aligned with what we find desirable. And so, at the very least, there is high potential for a fundamental disconnect between what would be desirable for a conscious being's experience and what a conscious being is likely to experience.

◆

We see the world not *as it is,* but *how it is* painted within the unique frame of our consciousness. Inexorably bound to our consciousness, our experience and understanding are always created by it, which was and is created by the natural world. The world thus exists behind a veil of subjectivism. In the words of the American author Eugene Thacker, from *In the Dust of This Planet:*

> The world-in-itself is a paradoxical concept; the moment we think it . . . it ceases to be the world-in-itself and becomes the world-for-us. . . .
>
> Even though there is something out there that is not the world-for-us, . . . this latter constitutes a horizon for thought, always receding just beyond the bounds of intelligibility.

All in all, this is not to suggest a solipsistic stance in which the physical world does not exist outside of our consciousness, but that the particular image of the world we have known and will forever be limited to knowing *is not that world.*

◆

Perhaps the primary and only real function of our consciousness is the ability to reflexively consider and become aware of consciousness itself. It is to show us *this*—to allow us to write, read, listen, think, ponder, and reflect on the nature of writing, reading, listening, thinking, pondering, and reflecting. It is only possible for a being to consider and understand what it means to have consciousness through consciousness, and thus, perhaps that is its one unique function—to enable the experience of self-awareness.

◆

The objective analysis of consciousness inherently always leaves out the essential subjective quality of it—what it is actually like to be conscious. Even if we were to understand the physical requirements of consciousness, where it comes from, and how it works, that still wouldn't explain or make sense of our experience of it. All definitions and theories of consciousness, both current and foreseeable, seem only to reveal an unresolvable dissonance between the experience of consciousness and what creates the experience. How does objective, lifeless, and physical matter form a singular, subjective, and self-aware experience? There appears to be something deeply inadequate about our sensibilities and logic as a means of understanding the nature of the very thing we are. In the words of American philosopher Thomas Nagel:

> If the subjective character of experience is fully comprehensible only from one point of view, then any shift to greater objectivity—that is, less attachment to a specific viewpoint—does not take us nearer to the real nature of the phenomenon: it takes us farther away from it.

◆

Consciousness is perhaps not something that can be looked at, but only through. Since all questioning, examining, and understanding of consciousness must be done through consciousness itself, this process is inherently self-referential, and thus, consciousness attempting to comprehend itself arrives at nothing. Evolutionary biologist and writer Richard Dawkins wrote in *The Selfish Gene:*

> Perhaps consciousness arises when the brain's simulation of the world becomes so complete that it must include a model of itself. . . . Another word for this might indeed be "self-awareness," but I don't find this a fully satisfying explanation of the evolution of consciousness, and this is only partly because it involves an infinite regress—if there is a model of the model, why not a model of the model of the model . . . ?

There is a fundamental circularity to consciousness. That is to say, consciousness itself can never be fully understood or conceived by consciousness.

◆

As a result of the reflexive nature of consciousness, consciousness appears destined to short-circuit when trying to understand itself. That's what humanity is. A short circuit, trying to understand itself.

◆

Consciousness is unknowable. Thus, we are all unknowable.

◆

Ultimately, we are all in something that we can seemingly only touch through a body and know through a conscious mind, forever prevented from contacting it outside of our personally filtered experience of it, forever limited to the methods of perception available to us, forever condemned to the persistent illusions that form as a result.

◆

We see the world as if it were ours to see. And yet outside of ourselves, *this world* does not even exist.

◆

The windows of our perception are also windows into our own minds. All perceptions are but perceptions of ourselves.

◆

The experience of consciousness—regardless of its origins, regardless of its functions, and regardless of its purpose—is an isolated experience.

The unbreachable nature of consciousness makes it impossible not only to understand its nature, but also, as the products and experiencers of its nature, it makes it impossible to understand ourselves. As individuals, our origins, our functions, and our purpose are unknowable. The totality of what we experience, what we think, and who we are is inaccessible. We are alienated not only from the world, but from ourselves. Self-awareness sets us in a raft on the sea of our being. There is seemingly unending water beneath us and an infinite space above us. We can't swim. We can't fly. We can only float. Aimlessly and alone.

◆

Everything we think and believe, everything we hope and are, is contained within that limited clump of matter inside our head. Everything that is beautiful and fascinating is found inside that, destined to shrivel back up and dissolve away into its origins.

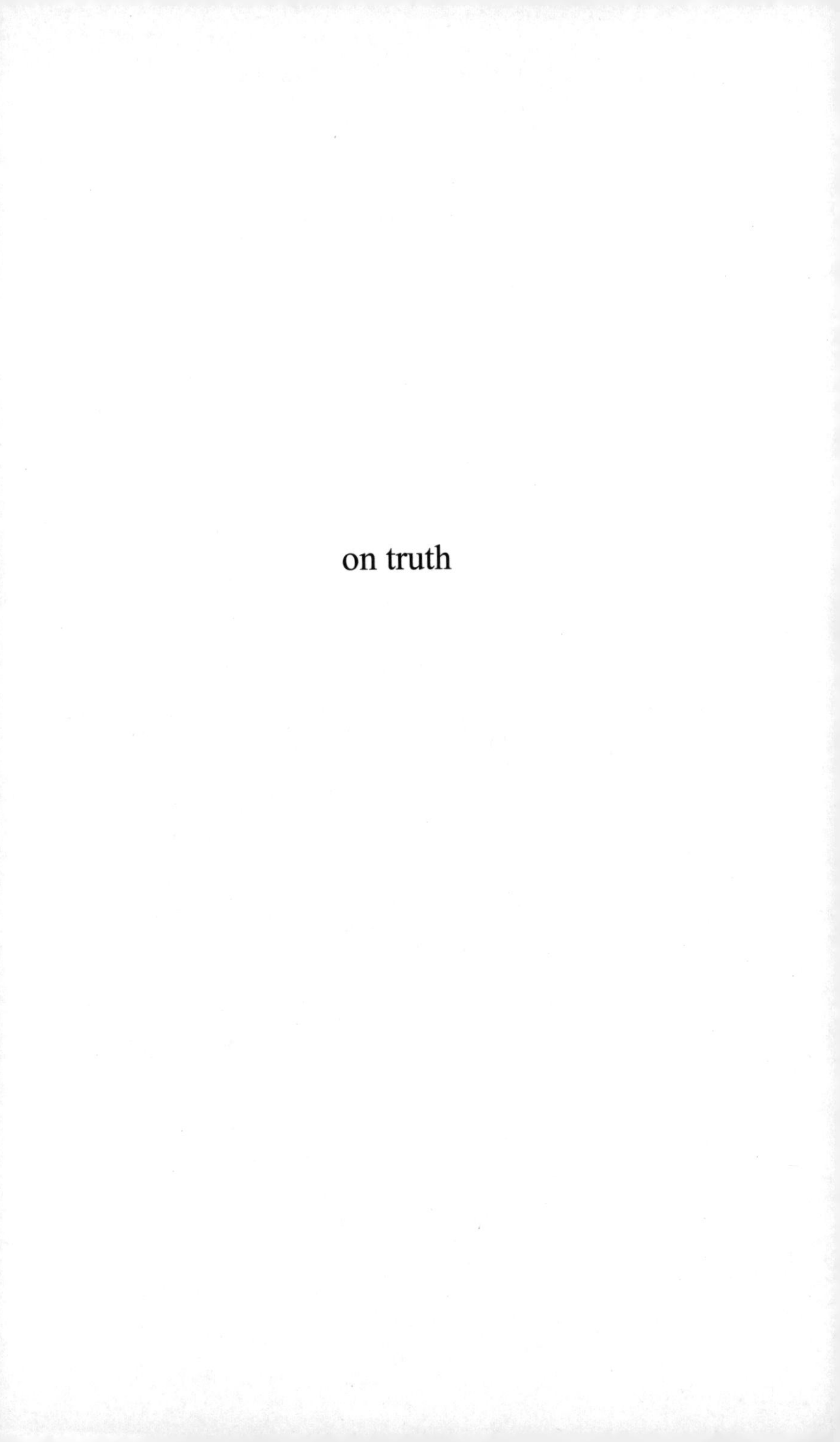

on truth

He wants to know how things work, what things are, and what they mean. He seeks all this knowledge not because he is inherently interested in it but because he wants to know things will be all right; and if they won't be all right, he wants to make them so.

When humanity speaks of truth, it speaks only of what it can see. It knows of nothing else. But, of course, truth exists beyond what humanity can see. In all likelihood, truth exists only beyond what humanity can see.

◆

We are stuck, lodged somewhere inside the crevices of our brain, incapable of ever thinking or perceiving from outside of it.

◆

The problem of truth is rooted in the problem of consciousness. Humanity does not appear capable of fully understanding the mechanisms of its consciousness, nor can it escape its consciousness. It does not understand the nature of consciousness, how or why it comes to be, what consciousness precisely does and permits, and so on. How can a being claim to fully understand what it is perceiving and thinking if it can't understand the total path through which it perceives and thinks? A being who cannot fully comprehend the mechanism by which it forms thoughts and knowledge—and can never test or know anything from outside this mechanism—can never know absolute truth. As the German theoretical physicist Max Planck put it, "Science cannot solve the ultimate mystery of nature. And that is because, in the last analysis, we ourselves are part of nature and therefore part of the mystery that we are trying to solve."

◆

The desire to find truth is a compulsion of consciousness, while the inability to ever know if one has found truth is an imperative of the relationship consciousness has with the natural world. We can never step outside of our consciousness to know what is beyond it, and thus we can never know what is true.

◆

Even the coldest and hardest-seeming of facts are discovered, interpreted, and understood through the subjective lens of an individual's consciousness—one limited to the time, place, and nature of its existence. Even if there is an objective truth to everything, how could any human being or group of human beings not be susceptible to misapprehending it through their limited, subjective modes of thinking?

◆

Events are real, but interpretations are always subjective. And events can only be *known* through interpretation.

◆

The very belief in an attainable objective truth is a subjective belief. Where does one go from there?

◆

Everything beyond our own existence—which is our only verifiable fact—is unknown and unknowable.

◆

From the character of a friend to the conditions of reality to the nature of ourselves, all we will ever know are the appearances. Underneath and inside—the truth—is something no one will ever know.

◆

There are no accurate ways to describe the truth. At best, it can potentially be pointed to with metaphor and art. But so-called objective, logical terms will always entirely miss the mark.

◆

Our awareness resides at the end of all the mechanisms and frameworks of perception and mental activity—our senses, our feelings, our languages, and our imaginations. We are a conscious observer trying to make sense of everything. But our cognition is limited and skewed, the process riddled with blind spots and biases—systematic errors in thinking formed out of the process of evolution, which always cares about survival and the ability to act but does not always care about accuracy and truth.

◆

There are so many blind spots in the mind, the mind is more like one big blind spot with one tiny spotlight.

◆

Who is to say the brain evolved toward accuracy and not deception? Evolution cares about accuracy only insofar as it is useful to survival. This alignment is likely both infrequent and limited.

The survival of the brain is a very different goal from the accuracy and dependability of the brain in the realm of abstract thought—in the realm of truth. Our brain's goals are very much misaligned with ours.

◆

We wield increasingly powerful tools, but all tools, no matter how powerful, are only as capable as the wielder. Humanity is its own bottleneck to true understanding.

◆

What is the desire for knowledge and truth if not a response to the fear of the unknown—and the desire to placate this fear? The desire for knowledge was thus born out of and driven by fear.

Ironically, and perhaps tragically, as we progress through our increasing knowledge propelled by our technologies and sciences, we become more aware of and sensitive to how much we don't know and may never know. We become more aware of and sensitive to the absurdity and uncertainty of life, death, meaning, the cosmos, and everything in between. And with this increasing awareness and sensitivity, we experience worse fear, dread, and anxiety. We love to make things worse for ourselves. It is a very special skill of humanity.

◆

What might we learn in the future that would change everything we think we know now? What will we never know that is fundamental to true understanding?

◆

Few people in history have believed their beliefs were wrong. But throughout history, how many people, groups, and societies have been right about much of anything? Civilizations' strongest-held beliefs have crumbled and fallen apart just like the pillars of their monuments. What does this suggest about the beliefs we currently hold? How do we reconcile the only clear lesson of history—that truth is a fine sand held loosely in the palm—with our convictions?

Our belief in our rightness has no bearing on its accuracy. In fact, history shows that, if anything, confidence indicates obscene wrongness. If we believe we are absolutely right about anything, we believe, with blatant disregard for the entire history of humanity, in a delusion.

◆

How long have we been wrong about nearly everything? How often have we looked back on our prior foolishness with condescension, proud to have surpassed our *unwitting* ancestors? Are we to believe that we are different, that we are special, that we are the first generation of the first species to have it mostly figured out?

The only thing clear across all stages of humanity is hubris.

◆

The more we progress, the smaller we become. The more we learn about ourselves and the universe, the more we realize how little we know and how little we matter. What we learn consumes us.

◆

We see only as far as we can, limited by the horizon of human capability at the time we exist. The frontier is infinite. And yet we will always be confined by it.

◆

Do we even want the truth if the truth will make us go mad?

Preference is rooted in one's belief about what will serve one best. Thus, the pursuit of truth is not really the pursuit of truth in and of itself, but rather, it is the pursuit of a preferred state of being—the belief that knowing the truth will ultimately grant a superior quality of existence. But will it? Has it? Does it?

◆

Does knowing what life is made of constitute a sacrifice of life itself?

◆

Humanity has developed sciences to understand things like the laws of nature, the foundations of life, and the phenomena of the mind. But has it not lost some degree of touch with all these things in the process?

We can travel into space, dissect and systematize the body, understand the science of happiness and the nature of nature itself, but do we not seem to be, in at least some respects, further from these things than ever? Perhaps a full experience of things like happiness, love, and life requires that we never fully understand them. Perhaps we have used our knowledge and reason to discover that happiness, love, and life exist at their purest when knowledge and reason are absent. But now, there is no turning back.

◆

We have broken the world into smaller and smaller parts, thinking that in doing so, it will become easier for us to see and understand the whole. But the puzzle that was once a solid image is now in millions of little pieces.

We can't make much sense of anything anymore.

◆

From the perspective of the truth seeker, life is a never-ending existential crisis.

◆

When you realize that the truth is made of glass, you finally stop throwing things at it.

◆

If there is any value to understanding the way things are, even just a little, it is in our ability to accept the way things are, including our potential ignorance and futility.

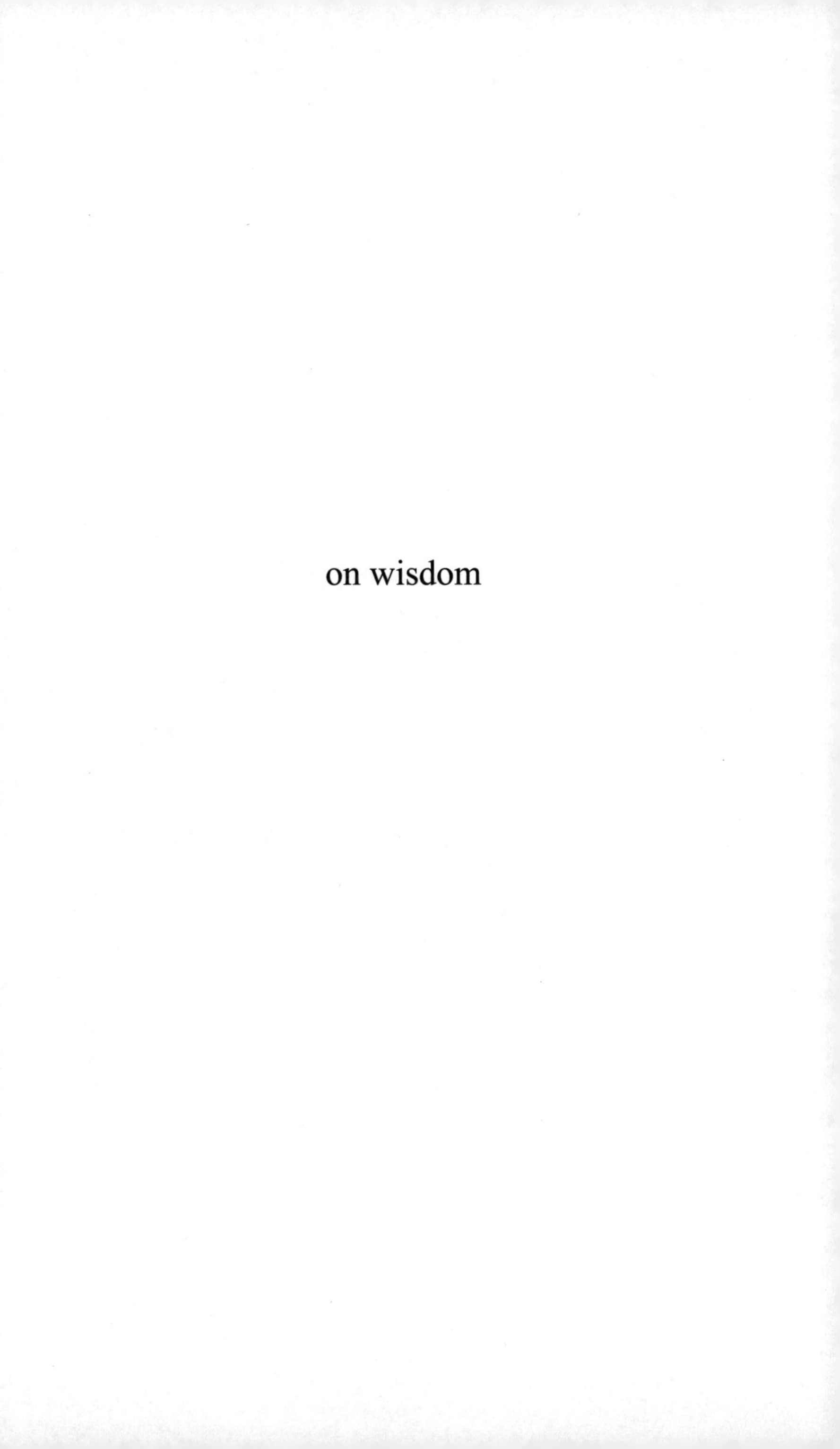

on wisdom

He has scoured so much of the world's information about how and how not to live, what and what not to do. And yet he has concluded very little—other than the fact that most of it contradicts. Notions sound nice when limited to particular circumstances, but when considered broadly, everything appears to mean nothing.

There are no absolutes.

He must accept his ignorance. To live with the self-awareness of his kind, he must embrace his unawareness.

Ignorance may or may not be bliss, but embracing one's ignorance is certainly wise.

◆

Ignorance is not found merely in the absence of knowledge, but also in the misdirection of knowledge.

◆

Life is filled with paradoxes. Life *is* a paradox. How does unconscious matter produce consciousness? How does lifeless matter birth life? How did anything come to exist in the first place? Has something always been, or did something once come from nothing? How can our existence be both meaningless and meaningful? How can things be both comprehensible and absurd?

We must love absurdity and paradoxes! We must embrace them! Nothing matters, and thus, this statement itself does not matter! In the words of Emil Cioran:

> When all the current reasons—moral, esthetic, religious, social, and so on—no longer guide one's life, how can one sustain life without succumbing to nothingness? Only by a connection with the absurd, by love of absolute uselessness, loving something which does not have substance but which simulates an illusion of life. I live because the mountains do not laugh and the worms do not sing.

◆

Paradoxes don't always need to be solved. Perhaps far more often and far more importantly, paradoxes are to be relished. We can stand on them to look out into where we can no longer see—a vista comprising a gradient of haziness turning into complete blackness. Just as we can appreciate a beautiful view of an immense landscape in nature, which words could never capture or express, we can stand quietly on these paradoxical cliffs and observe with awe and peace.

◆

It is perhaps the mark of true intelligence to know that opposing ideas and philosophies can and likely must exist inside the same head. Like a toolbox, the mind can and likely must retain various views and beliefs to sustain itself in a chaotic, changing, and ungraspable world. For every varying situation and context, one must adapt and use a unique instrument of interpretation and evaluation.

Each moment, physically and temporally, is its own world.

Contradiction is the norm. Consistency is performative at best.

◆

The greatest hypocrisy is criticism of hypocrisy itself.

◆

Wisdom is knowing the limits of wisdom—the limits of aphorisms and ideas, of these very words and of this very book, of all words and all books.

One can intellectualize everything, experience everything, read every book, scour every research paper, travel to every place, talk to every person, only to realize that the *answer* isn't out there.

There are enough ideas and clichés in the world to justify

nearly anything. All clichés and wisdoms are both true and false, meaningful and meaningless, depending on when and to what they are applied. Even the most brilliant thoughts and lines ever uttered or written inevitably face failure.

There is no advice, no person, no answer that could ever satisfy the question of how to live. There is no right way to live. No viable prescription, no correct answer, no guiding insight but this one: You are on your own in every moment, and each moment is created anew.

◆

To try to play God is to lose one's humanity.

◆

Wisdom belongs to those who can renounce their sense of importance and their assumptions of rightness and success. It belongs to those who replace these qualities with a universal compassion, a distrust in the self, and a radical humility.

◆

Exist for the time you have. Live decently. Try your best. Respect others and yourself. One does not need answers, or certainty, or comfort to live well. What is *yours* is wisdom. What is lived is true and real.

◆

We so easily forget how young we still are. The greatest, wisest, and most prudent members of humanity are still mere infants on the potential timeline of consciousness.

◆

History is, in large part, a conveyor belt of failed ideas. Time makes a fool out of all of us. All the most powerful thinkers in history have or will inevitably become expired objects in the warehouse of ancient artifacts.

◆

Ideals burn in humanity's hearth. We feed the fire with the kindling of so-called laws and truths derived from our plundering and dissection of nature. But this fire requires constant feeding. It is always on the brink of burning out—collectively and individually. Nothing can be discovered, nothing can be excavated, and nothing can be obtained that will keep the fire permanently lit and make the coldness of the universe go away. As long as we depend on the fire of truth and certainty, we will labor relentlessly to keep it going, and we will, in all likelihood, burn ourselves up with it.

◆

Humanity may be equipped with the weapon of reason, but it lacks the shield of self-reflection.

◆

To hate, to seek vengeance, to act on anger, to declare certainty, and to live with self-righteousness—all these things directly contradict the very nature of our existence and consciousness. We feel pain, fear, and anxiety not because there is a clear, single way, order, person, or group that has the answers or causes the problems, but because there isn't. There are no answers, no ways, no rights, no wrongs, no perpetrators. Only victims.

◆

Whatever we are certain of, we are almost certainly wrong. We have no clue what we have no clue of. None of us knows what's happening and why. The fear and anxiety this produces compel us to contrive a certainty we don't possess. We might look for a person, group, or belief that helps dampen our existential humiliation and paranoia. And if we believe we've found one, we will become entranced by it. We will become absorbed by it. We will fight to maintain and defend the person, group, or belief at all costs. And that cost will include us.

◆

No matter how much *clearer* things seem to become, one must never submit to belief or certainty. There is and will always be another cave to escape.

◆

Intellectual progress is found not by uncovering truths but by learning how to live well without them.

◆

We must learn how to be wrong, and to accept our wrongness, or we will loathe ourselves until the end. We must love and embrace the hypocrisy innate to humankind, or we will hate everyone. We must dial back our expectations and our dread of failure and futility, or we will always be the worst kind of miserable.

◆

To be aware is to attend constantly to our unawareness.

◆

The world needs more philosophy that sits outside the grand illusions of consciousness. It needs philosophy that does not pose or seek answers, does not provide resolutions or desire improvements, does not declare how or why to live, but rather, aids and comforts us all in the impossibility of achieving any of this; philosophy that presupposes and accommodates its inevitable contradictions.

on the peace of silence

He looks everywhere for the right words—the right words to describe everything, to define everything, and to know everything.

When he struggles to find what he's after, he continues to look for more words. He invents more words.

He speaks them louder and louder.

Soon, he yells. Then he screams.

The screams only echo, returning to him with no new insights. They're still just his words. They teach him nothing.

In between his screams and their echoes, he experiences silence. This is when, if he listens, he finds what he is after.

Most of what we feel, experience, and long for is beyond comprehension—beyond thoughts and words.

◆

Our origin is beyond thoughts and words. Our fate is beyond thoughts and words. Everything outside of us—the true nature of reality—is beyond thoughts and words.

◆

Our consciousness allows us to know that a realm exists beyond thoughts and words. We can comprehend the notion of the incomprehensible. We can know that there may be an infinite number of things we *cannot know.* In this, consciousness is the source of our disquiet about not only the unknown but the unknowable. At the same time it illuminates, it veils.

Worse, not only must we accept our unknowing, but we must deal with what we can *know* but can never fully articulate—the vague shadows and outlines we can point to but never quite grasp.

◆

There is so much that straddles the border of our comprehension—one leg in and one leg out.

◆

We all experience the haze of consciousness concealing the utter darkness beyond it.

◆

How much of what we experience (emotionally, sensorially, and abstractly) can never be truly *known* or articulated—by ourselves and others? Things we feel and *sort of know* but can never describe or pinpoint.

◆

How much has been experienced by individual humans for hundreds of thousands if not millions of years that will never be known by humanity collectively?

◆

How much could finally be known about ourselves in a hundred thousand years when or if the necessary words, concepts, and intellectual apparatuses are finally created—or discovered?

◆

No matter what the human psyche creates or discovers, its creations and discoveries will always be projections of itself contained and limited within itself. We may find better ways to understand and express ourselves, but we will never answer our longing to comprehend and integrate with what is beyond us—the *truth.*

◆

"Whereof one cannot speak, thereof one must be silent." With this line, Ludwig Wittgenstein reached with his words the very limit of what words can articulate about truth—the truth value of the absence of words.

When it comes to obtaining anything objective, absolute, or

final, where can one truly speak? To say nothing, to feel nothing, to know nothing—that is likely the closest one will ever come to the truth.

◆

There are times for noise and even screaming. And there are times for silence. We can embrace the dichotomy of noise and silence in our minds the same as we might in daily life. We can use our words and thoughts to engage with the world and each other, to have fun, to connect with our humanity and our capacity for thought. But we can also embrace silence and recognize how little often needs to be said, how simple things often can be, and how peaceful things often can feel.

◆

By more regularly inhabiting silence, by being willing to be "no one," and by relieving our voice, our presence, and our existence of constant involvement, we can find the kind of peace of simplicity and *correctness* we long for. The complexity of the world can almost melt away. Describing this silence and its profound clarity, Douglas Harding writes:

> It was all perfectly simple and plain and straightforward, beyond argument, thought, and words. There arose no questions, no reference beyond the experience itself, but only peace and a quiet joy, and the sensation of having dropped an intolerable burden.

◆

A loudness and confidence about one's beliefs does not indicate knowledge, but often a lack of awareness—of oneself and the complexity of the world. Alternatively, a sort of comfort with silence and the unknowability of everything indicates awareness—of one's own limits.

◆

Of course, by using words here, we are missing the point. One cannot espouse silence with words. One cannot capture the value or meaning of silence by capturing anything. One can never state the truth of what cannot be stated.

But one can espouse and capture a respect for silence—a willingness to be in it, when necessary. And one can advocate for the thoughtfulness, honesty, and modesty derived in honor of silence. That is what we are doing here.

◆

It is impossible to avoid having opinions and beliefs—and to keep from wanting to share those opinions and beliefs however we can. But *it is* possible to be more mindful of how we hold those opinions and more careful in how we express them.

◆

It's normal to want one's voice to be heard. It's normal to want to be perceived, liked, and followed. Having an impactful voice can be and often is a noble goal. But the point is, sometimes the greatest impact is silence. And we should want that, too.

◆

The world does not need more voices as much as it needs more careful voices.

on time and decay

Time is both his best friend and his worst enemy, depending on the moment.

Even as a friend, Time is brutal. It beats him up, gently enough at first, but consistently. A few friendly pushes to the ground don't hurt too badly, but over time, the cumulative effect of those pushes and pulls causes his joints to wither, his muscles to shrivel, his skin to sag, and his brain to rot. His once friend, his former source of joy, hope, and opportunity, turns on him fully and finally. When his body can take no more, Time pushes him to the ground once again, and this time, he does not get up.

For now, though, he is still standing. The friendship remains.

Time is often regarded as one of the most valuable things we can possess. It isn't really. What we truly value is the quality of our experience of it. Having more or less time makes no difference if our experience is poor—and our experience of time is largely contingent upon how we direct our attention. An individual lounging on the white sand beaches of Bermuda who is overtaken by anxiety about what they'll need to do when they return to their office or worksite, who is paying no attention to the warmth of the sun, the beauty of the ocean, the gentle breeze, or themselves, is worse off than an individual who, laboriously harvesting rice in a field, pays close attention to each stalk, each grain, each thought, each breath, reveling in the bluish morning light spilled with gold by the sun.

◆

In every moment, we decide what we want to pay attention to. Each moment contains a decision about how we direct our senses—what focal length and at what angle we direct the camera of our perception. But far more importantly, each moment also contains a decision about how we will watch what we capture—how we will process, interpret, and consider the media of our perception. Though what we experience and perceive is undoubtedly important, how we think about and consider what we experience and perceive is often far more influential to our experience of each moment. In the words of Sam Harris, "It's not so much what we pay attention to. It's the quality of attention. It's how we feel while doing it."

◆

A *good life* involves well-directed attention and well-received experiences.

◆

How we choose to spend our time (when we have a choice) is a declaration of our beliefs. It is the clearest declaration, representing what we believe about how a moment should be spent and a life should be lived. Of course, our beliefs can and do change across our lives, sometimes moment to moment, but if we are not living in alignment with our core beliefs, one of two things must be true: Either we don't realize what our beliefs are, or we lack the discipline to live according to them.

To discover what we believe, we must examine how we spend our time. To change our beliefs, we must change how we spend our time.

◆

Life is short isn't just a tired cliché; it's wrong. Sit quietly and do nothing for one minute. Life is a countless number of those. *Life is long.* We merely struggle to enjoy what we have before it's gone. That's not a matter of shortness. It's a matter of living ineptly.

◆

It is somehow possible to mourn the passage of time while also wishing the day would end.

◆

As time seems to speed up, life seems to slow down. There is less excitement and less fun.

Growing older brings more responsibility. We watch those around us disappear—in space and in time. We feel the pressure of finitude tighten in on us as the weight of past days increases.

◆

Consider a road trip. While on the road, as the hours pass, each hour becomes smaller and smaller in relation to the whole trip. With this, each new hour feels *different*. Pretty soon, the hours seem less and less *real*—or significant. They go by quicker, and we don't pay as much attention to them. Then, in the final stretch of the trip, we realize how close we are to the end, and a more lucid sense of time begins to return. The hours feel longer and longer. Soon, an hour becomes almost unendurable. At this point, you long to feel the fluidity and translucence of time again. But of course, we're not turning around. The only way is forward. And then, the trip ends.

◆

Eventually, we look in the mirror and realize that we don't recognize ourselves anymore. We are different. We are wearing the guise of age—which we don't remember putting on. Wrinkles. Grays. Bags. Weight. Dots. Speckles. Time.

We can't take any of it off.

◆

Our life has already flashed before our eyes. The moment we first open our eyes and light strikes our retinas, the shutter opens, and we begin to take everything in. From that moment on, in one continuous flash, we create our picture, trying to get everything in frame, trying to get our smile right, our hair right, our position right, the people right, the setting right. But there is only so much time. With each second, each day, each year, slowly but surely, the shutter closes, until eventually, it shuts.

If we want the image of our life to look and feel a certain way, we must get it in frame now.

◆

Everything must change. Everything must decay. Everything must end. The only constant is inconsistency. The only guarantee is finality.

on death and loss

Within the infinite space surrounding him, his finite end awaits him. Having lost any sort of belief in an afterlife, he knows that none of what he is or has is coming with him.

He soon joins everything else again.

There are two possibilities. Either we exist forever, or we die. And both are terrifying.

◆

Our subjective experience appears to exist solely by way of the physical mechanisms of a brain. So when our brains no longer function or exist, there is no longer any experience. No brain means no experiencer; no experiencer means no experience. In all likelihood, this is what comes after life for us. *Nothingness.* We dissolve back into the oneness of all things—beyond experience, beyond thought, and beyond comprehensibility.

◆

Death is the most significant moment of our lives (perhaps after birth), and yet we will never experience it.

◆

All values in life draw backward from death. Whether we realize it or not, death is at the center of and behind everything. It motivates all our subconscious and conscious behaviors. We are all running from it while running toward it, *deathly afraid.*

◆

It is not so much death that most of us are unsettled by, but rather, the unknown. Death is just the most extreme version of the unknown. It is beyond unknown; it is unknowable. *Something* can't ever know what it means to be *nothing*. To exist is to never know what it feels like to not exist. But to exist is to not exist, eventually. And to exist as a conscious, self-aware being is to know that this is your destiny. What a wonderful conundrum!

◆

To think about one's death is to think about something that exists beyond thought. It is to project oneself forward not only in time but in form—the form and shape of *nothingness*. This is, of course, completely nonsensical and impossible. Death, therefore, is something we can (and must) *know of* but can never *know*.

◆

In the loss of all things, we also lose the ability to experience loss itself.

◆

Whatever you do in life, whatever you beat and overcome, whatever you accomplish and obtain, however much safety and security you create, whoever you love and team up with, in one clean sweep, you will lose it all. How we bear the awareness of this condition is a wonder.

Everything humanity has done, in large part, has been directly proportional to the insanity, absurdity, and horror of this fact.

◆

Ironically, complaining about the tragedies of existence is something one would likely deeply miss if they *could miss anything* once they no longer existed.

◆

We must recognize and accept that every day is a battle against our life's enemy. And one day, no matter what we do, we will lose to this enemy. We cannot win the battle, but we can justify it; we can fight proudly and passionately. We can find the things and people that are worth dying for—people and things who will make the prospect of death and loss seem all the more unbearable.

We are like outnumbered soldiers, destined to lose terribly, but we proceed. Foolishness comes to mind first, but, upon further reflection, somehow, that foolishness exudes beauty and poignancy.

◆

We are, of course, not affected merely by the awareness of our own mortality, but also by the awareness of others' mortality. Those we love and those with whom we become intertwined—their deaths become partially our own. A part of us dies with everyone we lose.

◆

Why not just avoid investing in what will ultimately be lost or destroyed? The irony in that is this: If our concern is the loss of meaningful things, then in avoiding them altogether, we have already lost them. Worse, we never really experience them at all—at least not openly and deeply. Instead, we must accept and even revel in the inevitability of loss. As the poet Kahlil Gibran wrote, we must desire "to know the pain of too much tenderness . . . and to bleed willingly and joyfully."

◆

Worrying about the loss of things necessitates having something to lose. The pain we have felt, are feeling, and are worried about feeling in the face of terrible events is directly proportional to how much we love and care about the things in our life. Worry, fear, grief, and pain—these are not merely consequences of things gone wrong; they are also markers of what has gone right.

◆

To care about anything is to lose. To love anything is to be devastated.

◆

Worry, grief, loss, and pain are dependent variables in the equation of a well-lived life.

◆

The person nearest to you now, both physically and figuratively, will die. You know this. They know this. This fact ought to be the basis of every interaction we have with one another.

For this fact alone, we all deserve patience, kindness, and understanding.

◆

We are all uniquely bonded by our common plight: Not only will we die, but, as far as we know, we are the only creatures aware of this fact. What could bring us closer than knowing that we will all never know this existence again? In this, we are all one and the same. We all come from and are destined for the same nothingness.

◆

Through loss emerges an entire spectrum of boundless passion, desire, angst, sadness, happiness, and beauty to be had and experienced, the likes of which humanity has written about, sung about, created about, and loved because of since time immemorial.

◆

An awareness of death ought to make us love harder, say what we mean, be who we are, try what we want. And yet for most of us, it doesn't. If anything, it often does the opposite. This is perhaps the most tragic part.

◆

To suffer over insignificant things in the face of everything ending simply does not make sense. Every minor failure, misstep, argument, and so on is a mere drop in the bucket, destined to be poured out. We ought to fill the bucket with as many of our hopes, loves, and interests as we can—diluting our doubts and misfortunes while we still can.

◆

Life is risk. To live is to be afraid. What one does in response to this fear is what separates the living from the dead.

◆

People don't finish their lives. Lives finish people.

on futility

Slowly, all his favorite things and all his favorite people fade from his life—by disinterest, by distance, by death or disappearance. His passions, statuses, achievements, and possessions are lost, literally or to obsoletion. His physical and mental capacities diminish. He is alienated by the world as new generations become unfamiliar to him, and he to them. When things do finally begin to make a little sense, they collapse again into confusion or reveal themselves to be something else. He falls more and more in love with life, and then he loses it.

After traversing billions of years of chaos, random matter of the universe beat infinitesimal odds to form complex consciousness capable of comprehending itself and the stars from which it originated. And yet despite acquiring powers akin to those of a god, humanity now spends its days toiling away at tedious, ceaseless, mostly meaningless work with no end in sight.

◆

We have no endgame in mind, and yet we fervently and relentlessly dedicate immense time, effort, and sacrifice in the name of progress. But progress toward what? Surely, we know by now that no utopia awaits us—at least not for the human species.

◆

Aside from increased baseline health and safety, what has progress truly accomplished? These achievements are not trivial, but living longer and more securely in an existence devoid of psychological prosperity is hardly meaningful progress.

◆

Humanity's endless desire for control, optimization, production, scale, and automation serves no purpose other than to kick the can down the road, prolonging the suffering for future generations. In the words of the historian Yuval Noah Harari, from *Sapiens:*

> We have mastered our surroundings, increased food production, built cities, established empires and created far-flung trade networks. But did we decrease the amount of suffering in the world? . . . Despite the astonishing things

> that humans are capable of doing, we remain unsure of our goals and we seem to be as discontented as ever. . . . Is there anything more dangerous than dissatisfied and irresponsible gods who don't know what they want?

◆

The world is run by people who don't know what they need or who they are.

◆

Humanity has fanatically and haphazardly run down an unending hallway, opening every door in hopes that one will have something inside. The rooms are all empty—and have been from the start. The only thing that is full is humanity's unrelenting imagination—its ability to envision rooms filled with glory and salvation despite no evidence of either.

◆

Humanity has spent its entire existence striving and waiting for something unknown, trying nearly everything it can to get it. And yet here we are, seventy thousand years in, and we still don't know what we are striving and waiting for. Little has come of our endurance in the way of answers, clarity, wisdom, or sustainability. We remain clueless as to what it is or could be that will gratify us. And so we continue striving and waiting.

◆

The world propels itself through some *will*—to life, power, decay, or something else. Everything exists and operates through us and in spite of us. The world makes tools of us to aid an existential order it simultaneously hides from us.

We are pawns—happy pawns—willing to sauté ourselves with a smile if that's what the universe ordered for lunch.

◆

For every peak humanity has reached or created, it has extracted a giant clump of Earth in the process.

Every peak creates a new valley.

◆

From every peak humanity has reached or created, we continually see nothing.

◆

Hope is humanity's venom. In its fervor for consumption and conquest in the name of utopian ideals, it bites and infects other creatures. In its thrashing agitation and need for predominance, it doesn't realize it has also caught, bitten, and infected itself, paralyzing itself in its own absurdity.

◆

No other species and no other generation of humanity have ever had to see the absurdity, chaos, and horrors of existence in such clear resolution, all at once, all the time.

Every new generation gets the pleasure of seeing everything in clearer, crisper resolution. Coming soon to existence: *the most graphic and tragic film ever made in 10K VR!*

◆

For a long time, humanity was the leading species of the world—the showrunner. Soon, it will be the stagehand.

◆

It has never been clearer that humanity does not own itself.

◆

Hopefully, the robots can solve everything, and we can feel like the parents who could never achieve what their children go on to do—obtain peace, truth, and salvation—and claim it as our own.

◆

The world is messy and unclear. The cosmos is a hellfire of chaos from which we are born and into which we are thrown. Perhaps we are not purifying agents but instruments of the universe's chaos, deluded by the coping mechanism of rationality into thinking that we can offer something different.

We unknowingly carry out the universe's dirty work, trying to extinguish a fire while fully engulfed ourselves.

◆

The primary commodity produced by humanity is *anesthesia.*

We awoke in the middle of evolution's surgery, and the human project is one lifelong endeavor to deal with the pain. We are sliced open, exposed, gruesome, and heinous. Everything we do and work toward is designed to keep us from knowing and feeling this. Keeping relentlessly busy doesn't take the pain away, but it prevents the mind from experiencing it. And so the suffering of existence becomes *painless*—and continuing on seems reasonable.

◆

Madness is knowing that life is inherently disappointing and impossible to resolve, yet still expecting the opposite. Thus, the entire human project is madness.

◆

The imaginary goalposts of life are constantly being moved away from us, and we're too afraid to admit that even if we score, it won't change the outcome of the game.

◆

We were set up, forced into something with no clear, good way of doing it, deluded into believing we can do better.

◆

An individual who dedicates their life solely to their accomplishments must face the failure of all accomplishments.

◆

Moments of achievement are mostly just a brief reprieve from the pain of all our missteps and losses.

◆

We will all be replaced—by others, by technology, by progress. The days when we had to explain how things worked to those older than us become the days when we need the explaining. Soon, the explaining becomes futile. Soon, everything becomes futile. At some point, none of us will be important in the ways we once were, in the ways we once longed and fought for. This goes for each of us and all of us—the entire endeavor of human consciousness. Every new technology we don't understand, every joke we don't get, every popular thing or place we haven't heard about intones our ultimate obsolescence.

◆

At some point in the distant future, no matter how things go or how well we do as members of our species in the relay race of existence, almost certainly, all life and sentience will become the smoke of a candle long since burned out with no one around to smell its fragrance.

◆

The world goes about its business as if everything weren't on a conveyer belt heading straight for the void. We are all grabbing at nothing and trampling each other along the way.

◆

We live inside the simple anxiety of endless to-dos on a path with no real consolation.

The only salvation, it seems, is to renounce it all; to slow to a near halt; to look closely at the leaves and long for the stars.

It may all be for nothing, but in moments of wonder, perhaps it is worth it all.

◆

If humanity is to improve, it must first attempt to free itself of its delusions. It must renounce the self, deny its desire for progress, its thirst for success and resolution, its belief in itself.

Of course, this is all impossible.

◆

No real stories end well.

◆

The tragedy of humanity becomes almost endearing when considered with a sort of sympathy. The human project is like a young child trying to lift something far too heavy for them. It is not tragic; it's adorable and touching.

◆

It is as if the train of human existence is on a track, heading toward a wall. We keep shoveling coal into it. If we had any sense, we would stop the train. But we can't. What would we do then?

We cannot conceive of a life where the train stops moving. It goes against everything we are—what we are made of and by. And so we keep going.

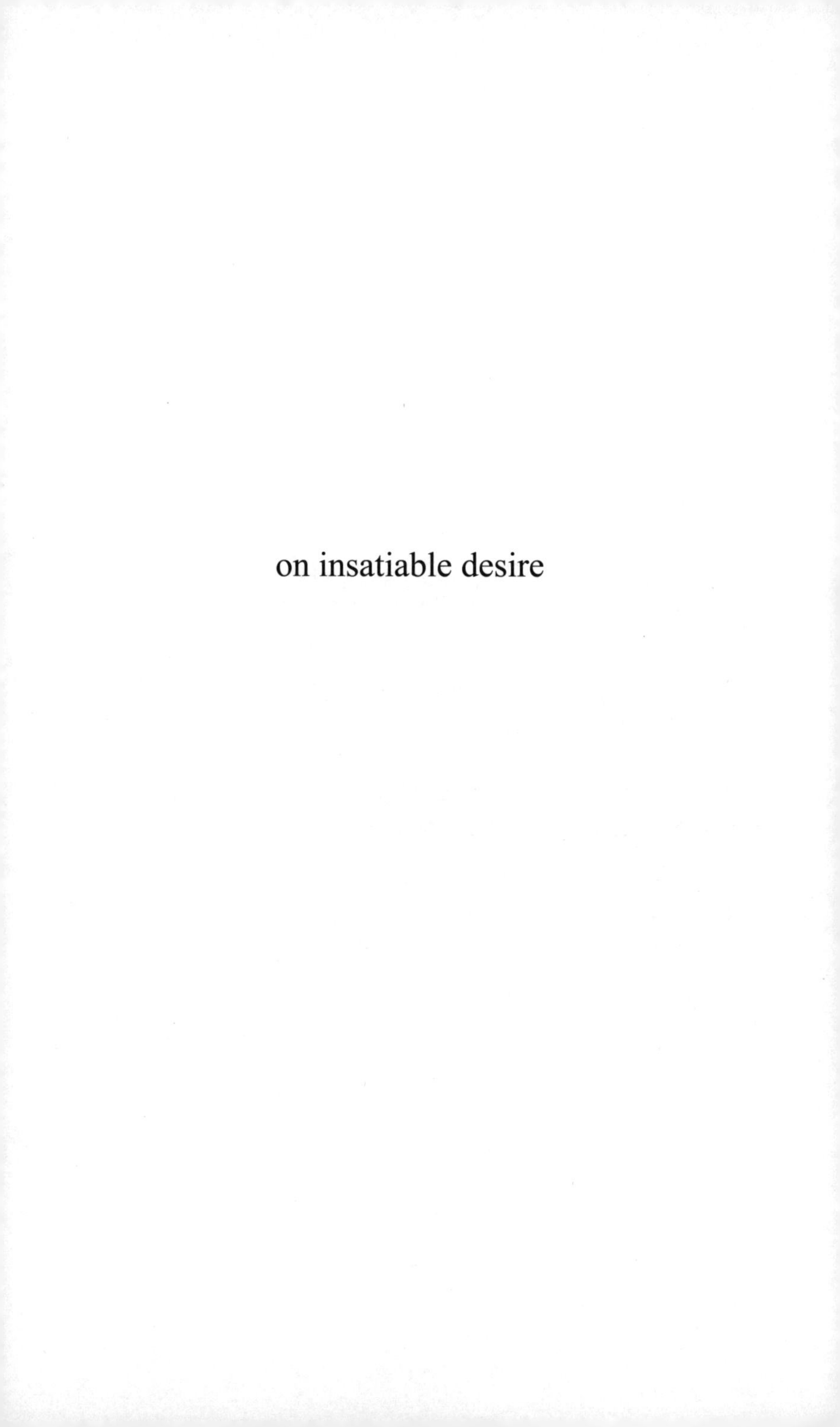

on insatiable desire

His desire causes him suffering. In seeking to satisfy and escape his desire, he only exhibits more desire. He has tried everything—both inward and outward, material and immaterial. But nothing has worked, and he continues to look for and try anything he can.

Even the desire to no longer desire is itself a desire. Thus, he is forever caught in a feedback loop of desire. Thus, he is forever caught in a feedback loop of suffering.

Here the world floats, basking in its glory, just as miserable and unsatisfied as when it began!

◆

There is a kind of misery in this world that has no real reason. It cannot be rationalized, solved, or otherwise redirected. It's simply par for the course.

◆

Every new species is born out of and into suffering. What is evolution if not life trying to outrun and escape its own horrific conditions? Isn't nearly every evolutionary adaptation an attempt to be consumed less and to consume better? All forward motion through life and evolution is motivated by the desire to escape suffering—suffering inflicted by the Earth, the body, or other beings. And yet, as history and the state of all things have shown, suffering cannot be escaped in life. It is a fundamental property of existence. The prospect of being destroyed or consumed motivates a striving to overcome these conditions, and this striving, in turn, breeds its own new kind of suffering. Ultimately, evolution leads to new conditions in which being destroyed and consumed can and will persist.

Suffering is not a bug of evolution; it is a feature.

◆

All things strive. To be alive is to strive. To be conscious is to be aware of that striving. To be aware of that striving is to be constantly tormented by the nature of life.

◆

Having climbed the ranks of all other life on Earth, humanity has reached the point where its greatest predator is itself. It has escaped all major animalistic threats, only to find that the fuel of suffering and striving persists within. Humanity has found and created new ways to suffer, victimizing itself both individually and collectively. The body, the brain, the Earth, and the cosmos still work to devour the human being in order to propel some forward motion.

◆

The human mind is not wired for happiness. The experiencer of the human mind was not considered by the processes that built it. Evolution cares about survival and action. If that means the experiencers of its creations are often absurd and miserable, both in pain and yet incapable of easily terminating themselves, fueled by an impossible, eternally insatiable desire to end all desire, then so be it!

◆

The tightrope of existence is walked from birth to death, suspended above depths of reasonlessness misery.

Don't look down.

◆

In response to the fundamental, universal suffering of all living things, given the apparent power to try to understand and control reality—which is ultimately always to no avail—humanity creates its own special kind of suffering.

◆

We seem to possess an infinite supply of dissatisfaction. It is humanity's number one export and import. We feast on it endlessly.

◆

Our ideals, our logic, our desire to placate everything that inflicts us becomes that which inflicts us.

◆

Humanity resembles a chained-up animal that is willing to bite its own limbs off to become free. But its limbs are part of its chains.

◆

In striving for perfection and eternity, in clinging to things, we are inevitably at odds with how everything works.

◆

How many shimmering pools must we reach in the desert of life before realizing there is no water? How many times must we learn this, only to keep chasing more?

Apparently, what we are really after is the continual pursuit of mirages. There is no other reasonable explanation. We seem to like—*love*—the disillusionment of arriving repeatedly at dry sand. Our desire for contentment is itself a mirage. We desire *desire*.

◆

When we feel happiness, it can almost trouble us, as if something isn't right, intimating an end—a sort of death.

What we seem to prefer, rather than happiness, is the strange, paradoxical comfort of misery's discomfort; the discontent of agitated striving.

◆

What is left to do if all things are good—if all things are satisfied? For what reason will I do anything if I am totally and completely happy with the way things are?

◆

By never satisfying our discrete desires, we satisfy our ultimate desire—to continue desiring. We need our discontent to persist.

◆

To want to not want is still a want. To choose to do nothing is still to do something. There is no escape—not even through renunciation or asceticism.

◆

Perhaps it is the natural order to try to force things, to cling to things, to conceive of things, to judge things, to make things *worse*.

Humanity is part and parcel of the whole of nature, but our intervention in nature is often seen as separate—as unnatural. How could this be? Human, conscious efforts, however seemingly harmful or forceful or unnatural, stem from the same force of nature as everything else. Humanity is not separate. Not exempt. Everything it does, it is compelled to do by nature. Its destruction of nature, its seeming conflict and struggle against nature, *is natural*. Nature is simply *destructive*.

◆

To act in what seems like opposition to nature is always in accordance with it. Everything is a different mode of nature. To oppose nature is nature opposing itself, which is still nature *naturing* just the same.

No one can escape the natural order—not through desire, nor through the extermination of desire.

◆

We think we seek happiness. We think we seek freedom. But what we really seek is the struggle toward both. We seek, not by choice but by necessity, suffering.

◆

The safest way to avoid misery is to realize your taste for it.

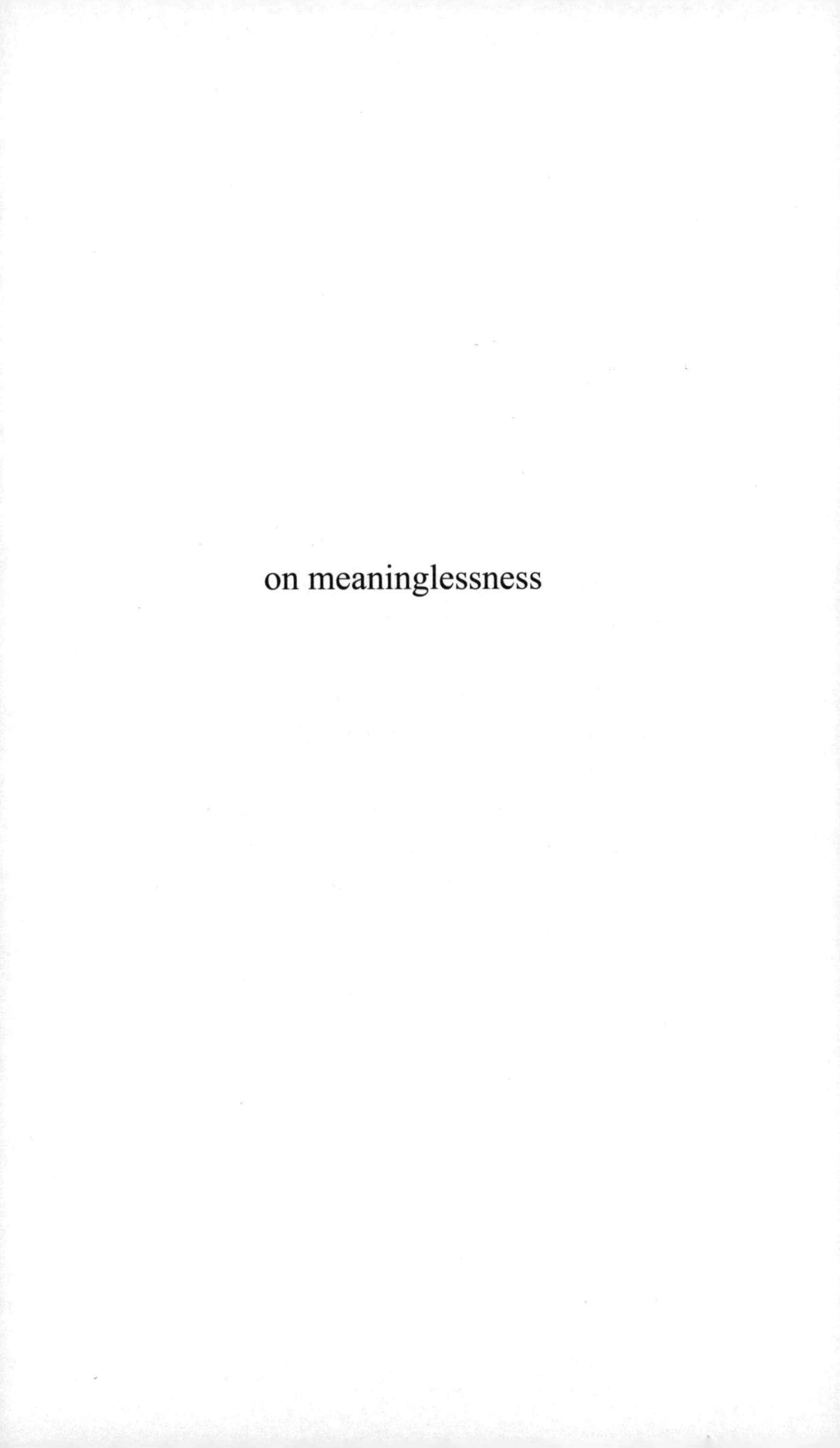

on meaninglessness

He was brought into this world for reasons that were not his own, reasons that did not have him in mind, reasons that did not serve or regard his experience. He did not exist prior to being conceived. How could his conception have regarded him as a reason? His birth is the biggest choice of his life, and he never made it. Likewise, the process and reality through which he exists do not regard him or his reasons. There are no reasons. The origins of his existence preceded reason itself. Now, he scrambles, trying to find them, to create them.

When one realizes that life is inevitably suffering and that lasting happiness is impossible, one is left to wonder: *What is the point?* Finding no point, one is left to ask: *Why suffer for no reason?* Humanity's plight lies in these two questions. Life is undeniably riddled with suffering, and this suffering appears to lack any intrinsic justification.

◆

The human being feels as though he is at the center of everything. He feels he is important, thus he needs to *be* important. But when he realizes that he is not the center of everything and likely not important to anything or anyone beyond himself, what is left for him? A fundamental contradiction between what he needs and what *is true*.

◆

For as long as humanity has looked out at the cosmos and wondered about its importance—yearned for its importance—it has been destined for torment.

◆

We are a zit on the body of an infinite organism, destined to *pop*.

◆

Religion has long been where the meaning of life is derived. If the Abrahamic religions are true, and a god did create this universe, then there is an intended purpose for us and life. All is well!

The problem is that the attempts of religion to define and argue for this case, to reveal this purpose, appear incoherent.

The further along we move in our understanding and capabilities as a species, the further behind religion seems to trail. Religion appears to be humanity's elderly, senile grandparent, trying to keep up—wise in spirit but fumbling in its grasp of the present.

◆

Religion requires faith. Faith is ultimately the belief in something without evidence or coherence. Who would claim this as an answer to anything? Everything, then, is an answer! I have faith, yes! I have faith in the Flying Spaghetti Monster!

◆

In a universe where the magic depends solely on where you are sitting in the theater, all gods are charlatans.

◆

For human life to have some true, objective purpose, that purpose must exist beyond humanity. Humanity must be able to point to or signify something outside itself. Humanity appears, however, unable to do this.

At best, we have access to the narrow realm of meaning created by our actions, our choices, and our subjective definitions of life. This is not trivial or *meaningless,* but it is not what humanity fundamentally longs for when it shouts and strives for purpose. Humanity's fundamental desire for meaning is for true, objective meaning—the sort by which one can determine actions, choices, and definitions, rather than the other way around. We need something outside ourselves—a reference point of objective purpose to calibrate and make sense of our meaning. But this objective purpose is, at best, inaccessible, and, at worst, nonexistent. There is nothing for us to point to. Unless science somehow discovers a god or godlike force with a clear plan and order that meaningfully involves us, there doesn't appear to be any possible scenario in which there is or would be some external reference point of purpose. How could there be?

We cannot create the meaning or purpose of life outside ourselves, and it is philosophically dishonest to claim that, without this, we have found life's meaning and have satisfied our fundamental yearning.

◆

Albert Camus spoke of faith in the religious sense as a sort of philosophical suicide. Yet in his philosophical essay *The Myth of Sisyphus,* he says we must imagine Sisyphus, a king in Greek mythology condemned to eternally roll a boulder up a hill for no reason, to be happy. Is this not faith? Why should we imagine or believe that Sisyphus is happy if there is no evidence for this and it is incoherent?

We want more than the individual meaning and purpose we imagine for ourselves; we want more than to imagine we are happy; we want to be meaningfully part of a grand, lucid, and objective purpose beyond ourselves; we want the boulder to go somewhere else, to mean something else.

If we can create meaning for ourselves, we should. But it is naïve to assume or claim that any personal, individual meaning satisfies the fundamental human yearning for *true meaning.*

◆

It doesn't help to imagine anything. At some point, you have to actually *know* it yourself. This is the fatal flaw of all religions, of all doctrines, of all hope. They are built on imagination—and faith in the imagined. No truly discerning individual believes, deep down, in what they have never and can never see or know.

◆

How can one maintain a life-affirming attitude if their view of life is not affirmative?

If one sees life as negative or meaningless, any interpretation placed on such a foundation returns one to where one began—in need of some truth or meaning beyond themselves, something other than what one sees and experiences. Thus, one is caught in a feedback loop of negation, spiraling into the abyss.

◆

Perhaps in our *killing of God*—which Friedrich Nietzsche wrote about nearly one hundred fifty years ago when he warned of humanity's decaying faith in religious ideals—we did not simply destroy the structure of meaning, but we dissolved the very material of meaning. The material and debris once used to cover the void of our existence are not simply broken and scattered around, able to be recycled into new forms. No, they have been dissolved away completely. It was all an illusion.

◆

We attempt to make our reasons out of everything, but the universe makes jokes out of our reasons.

◆

The events of our lives don't need reasons. We need reasons.

◆

There appear to be no destinations or reasons for us.

Maybe there are, but we will never know or reach them. Maybe there are, but they are all behind us, and nothing ahead will make it make sense now.

◆

The true story of the universe is written with invisible ink in a self-destructing book that kills its readers.

◆

Our beliefs won't save us, no matter how hard we believe in them.

on nihilism

The more time that passes, the more places he visits, and the more people he meets, the more he comes to feel that there's nothing much out there. It's all in his head, and hopefully in the heads of a few others who occasionally let him in.

There is an escape hatch to meaninglessness, crafted by meaninglessness itself. When taken to its conclusion, to a philosophy of nihilism, meaninglessness itself becomes meaningless.

If *everything is meaningless,* then so too is this declaration. The same feedback loop that traps humanity in the abyss also weaves a safety net that catches it.

A true nihilist goes the full distance. They use nihilism to deny and negate nihilism itself. Nothing formed, believed, or said adequately tracks onto reality, including nihilism.

To believe in nothing is to believe in something. To hold the value that all values are baseless is to deny one value with another. It is a paradox that cannot be escaped. Humanity is a paradox that cannot be escaped. We are meaning-creating machines who, in attempting to prove and execute a total negation of all meaning, cannot help but do the opposite.

Humanity must create meaning, for it has no choice.

◆

Nihilism is profoundly egocentric, and profoundly human. There is perhaps nothing more obnoxiously human than to declare that, since humanity cannot find some grand meaning for itself, everything must be meaningless.

◆

Fundamentally, what does meaning mean? Why do we need it? Why do we need things to have meaning? What are the implications of this requirement? No other beings seem to need meaning—at least not in the conceptual form we do. For other beings, the meaning of life appears to be simply life itself. But humanity, living as it does in the abstract realm of its consciousness, hovers above, assesses and evaluates, and conceives of absurd concepts like meaninglessness.

Consciousness has come so far and can achieve so much, and yet it has left behind what is so simply and plainly obvious: Life is the purpose of life.

◆

Life is the meaning of life. Thus, like measuring a minute with a minute or an inch with an inch, the concept of the meaning of life does not produce anything beyond itself because it is incoherent as a means of measurement.

◆

Just as the scientific explanation of music is not melodic, and the scientific explanation of humor is not funny, perhaps the scientific explanation of the meaning of life is not meaningful.

◆

If we don't know and perhaps can never know the true, objective meaning of existence—and whether there even is one—perhaps we ought to exhibit a sort of agnosticism regarding it. Perhaps there is a meaning. Perhaps not. Perhaps we are part of that meaning. Perhaps not. Perhaps we can understand it. Perhaps not. As the twentieth-century playwright Samuel Beckett said of his plays, the key word is *perhaps*.

on madness

Most of the world is beyond his awareness. Much of what he is is beyond his awareness. And yet he expects himself to fully understand things and to act as if he does.

He did not choose his existence—his body, mind, or circumstances. He does not fundamentally control any aspects of them. These conditions are inextricably linked with chaos and suffering. And yet he expects himself to sit quietly, behave amicably, and go about his life calmly and lucidly as if everything were okay.

He works so hard to keep his madness at bay. But he is mad. His madness precedes him. Hiding it, running from it, and denying it are three of its features.

We are awakened into chaos and expected to act as though everything is in order.

The cosmos is not madness. Madness is the fact that humanity expects itself to act like everything is fine when it is not.

◆

Every one of us possesses thoughts, desires, compulsions, and behaviors (realized or unrealized) that are, by all general standards, completely insane. Yet we must act as if this is not the case. We all must play along.

We are characters thrown onto a stage with no script, told to make it work. The plot makes no sense. Our character is mad. The dialogue is forced. The whole thing is infuriating.

◆

So many of our thoughts lie in a fetal position inside our heads—or they run around aimlessly, screaming to no end. Yet if we are to coexist with others in a civilized society, these innermost thoughts and feelings, which we neither fully understand nor control, must be ignored. We learn to hide them away not because this resolves them, but because letting them into the daylight to blow off steam might render us mad.

◆

It is a unique kind of madness to have a mind that finds purpose in its own torment, in a world that offers it nothing, among a society too exhausted to engage with it. The expectation of sanity in such a condition is perhaps the clearest example of humanity's madness. The call for sanity is itself insanity.

◆

The older and supposedly *saner* we become, the *madder* we become.

The loss of our innocence and youth marks the death of our sanity—not because we were sane as children, but because adulthood suddenly demands that we *play sane.* A child spouting gibberish or running around with an imaginary friend is seen as natural and adorable; an adult doing the same is considered mad. And so sanity dies when the possibility and standard for insanity is born.

Madness is not merely running around talking to oneself; it is the compulsion to do so (to engage in any *childlike behavior*) confronted by the expectation that such behavior is unacceptable.

The child in us must die, but we never cease grieving them. We grieve our whole lives—quietly and to ourselves.

◆

The experience of existence's maddening nature is like being poked millions of times: The intensity of each poke remains constant, but the irritation it causes gets so much worse over time.

Eventually, we have no choice but to go numb.

◆

How many times must we experience the strongest love fall flat, the best friendships disappear, and the most obvious truths collapse? How often must we witness empires rise only to be destroyed, their societies pillaged? How many times must we create new problems with technologies designed to solve old ones? How often must we fight and kill over the wrong-sounding noises and the wrong-looking colors? How many times must we feel the failure of being and the futility of triumph before we realize we are insane?

◆

We act out of madness to avoid our madness, projecting it onto the world.

◆

Only a particularly mad species can watch its loved ones die, pleading in horror, and then think, *Ah, I will bring more life into this world! I will fall in love again!*

◆

We are all composed of and live within the electrical firings and chemical compounds of a brain trying to map a self onto an unstable universe. We sit at the center of this chaos, trying to narrow a molecular ocean into a tiny canal. Successfully navigating so-called "sane" human life is as miraculous as being itself. Every moment of success, every right action, every congenial encounter is a wonder that defies everything one would expect.

◆

There is wisdom in a sort of general madness—a wisdom that informs us not to act with grandeur, but to let it all go. It shows us there are no right paths or set directions; everything is up in the air; the world is anything and nothing. "I would like to go mad on one condition," wrote Emil Cioran, "namely, that I would become a happy madman, lively and always in a good mood, without any troubles and obsessions, laughing senselessly from morning to night."

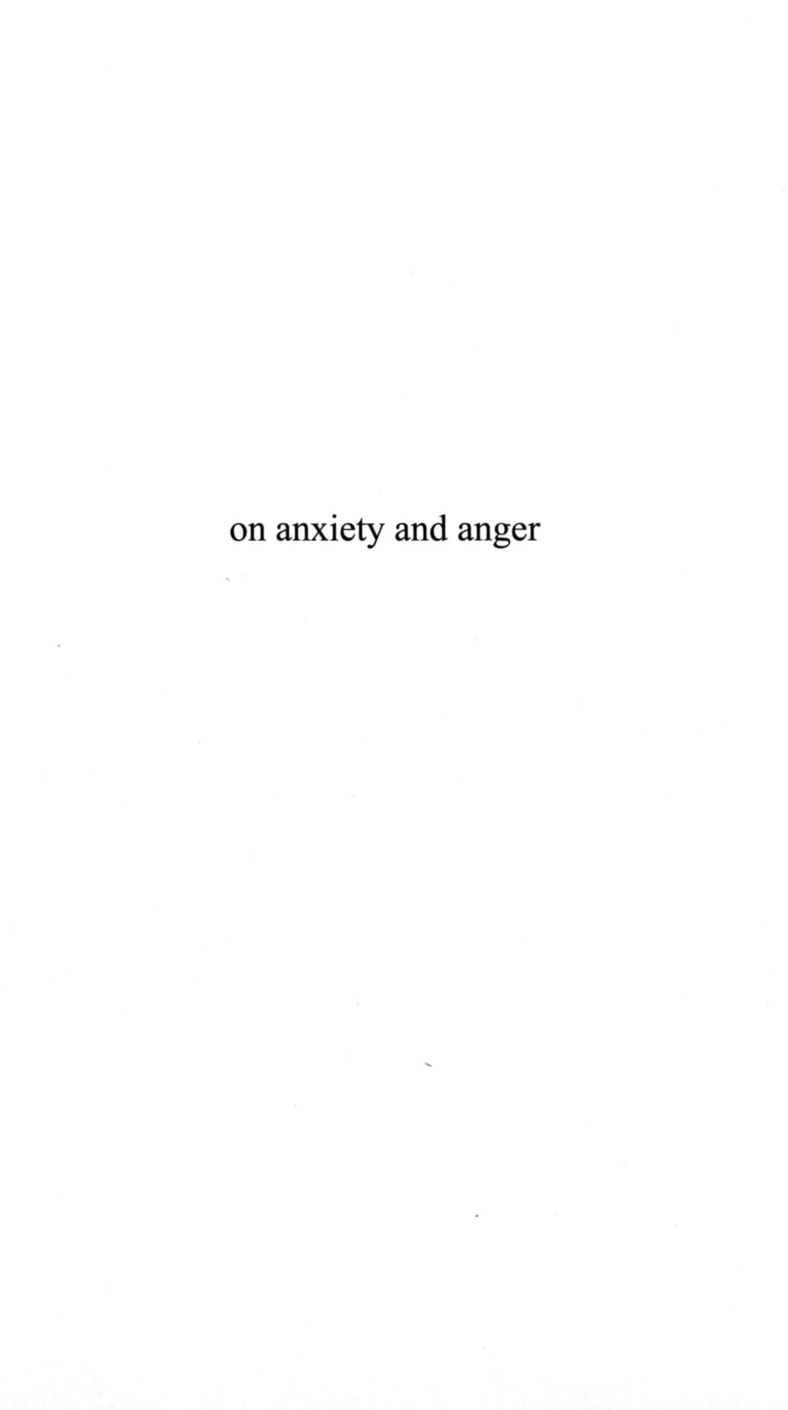

on anxiety and anger

He can see and comprehend the world as it plays out. He can reflect on the past and imagine the future. In some ways, he can predict the future—but only a tiny bit and only some of the time. Mostly, however, everything is out of his control. Things go how they go. And he watches—powerless and deserted.

He wants everything to go well, to go his way. But very little does.

For the human being, there is no living without thinking. And there is no thinking without worrying.

◆

As conscious beings, we possess foresight—the ability to imagine, consider, evaluate, and predict what will happen in the future. This ability gives us many advantages. It allows us to plan and prepare, to build things that will last, and to imagine and hope. But also, of course, this foresight comes with a terrible curse. It makes us aware of the things that can and will go wrong. Far worse, though our foresight is deeply impressive, it is simultaneously deeply limited. It allows us to know that things will go wrong but prohibits us from ever truly knowing how or when. We must live between possibility and certainty. That is anxiety.

◆

In every moment, we face the unknown and must decide what to do with it. We are filters through which the future becomes the past. Behind every decision is a different state of being, a different course of life, a different condition of the world. In nearly every conscious moment, we stand at the intersection of past and future as a crossing guard for the infinite possibilities of life. Our responsibility is immense, yet our foresight is limited. How could we *not* worry constantly? A moment free of worry is a blessing of ignorance.

◆

We want calm in a chaotic world, safety in a fragile body, peace and certainty in a mysterious, fluctuating, indifferent universe.

We want the impossible and endure the consequences: intense anxiety and despair.

◆

We are mostly ignorant of all the things that should concern us, and yet, there is still so, so much to be anxious about.

◆

There are so many qualities of life we want to avoid, eradicate, or pretend don't exist. And we love to worry about them relentlessly, compounding their negative effects. We so often worry about problems before they arise—or despite their never being a real threat.

◆

We unnecessarily focus on negative things, even though we know this makes us miserable. Here, we find the dichotomy between a body and brain evolved for survival and the often-helpless byproduct of self-awareness. No matter how aware we are of our superfluous anxiety, foolishness, and negativity, they largely persist. Though we no longer need to be as hyper-aware or fixated on negative stimuli as our ancient ancestors were, we mostly are. So much of us is beyond our understanding and control, comprising countless functions derived from our ancestors, whose misery saved them. Now, it *kills* us.

◆

We are burdened by our consciousness with a deep awareness of the future. We find ourselves stuck between the finite and the infinite, the now and the not-yet, unable to reconcile either. Every moment is lubricated with the perpetual slipperiness of impossibility.

To make the most of the present requires sacrificing some part of the future. To preserve the future requires sacrificing some part of the present. To be human is to desire both, forced to live in between, never fully grasping either.

Wisdom lies in accepting this condition.

Lower your expectations and live with a touch of pessimism, and the occasional good will emerge.

◆

The anxiety involved in decision-making stems from the realization that we don't truly understand why we choose the things we do. Our decisions come from *us,* but we don't know where *we* come from.

◆

Things always seem to go to plan when you don't have one.

◆

Without possibility, there would be no anxiety. Conversely, without anxiety, there would be no possibility.

◆

How does one determine whether worrying is useful or detrimental? Only by worrying about worrying.

Telling oneself to stop worrying tends to have the inverse effect. One might easily begin worrying about worrying and then worrying about how they can't stop, only making the whole thing worse. Once worry begins, in some sense, it's already too late.

We are all trapped in some amount of unnecessary worry. Accept this, and perhaps the worry will occasionally wane.

He uses anger to disguise his weakness and create an illusion of strength. While anger makes him feel strong, it diminishes his intelligence and resilience.

His true strength comes from a kind of passivity, like water that flows and bends around boulders, eroding them into pebbles.

Anger arises from our unfulfilled desire for control. The universe rejects our desire and controls itself. And we become angry.

◆

In moments of anger, we confront how incapable we are—how meager and weak. Anger creates an illusion of unfeeling strength, a desperate attempt to match the universe in its indifference and aggression. We fight, scream, thrash, and throw things. But the Earth, the air, and the cosmos feel nothing. We feel the pain.

◆

There are so many reasons to be angry, but only a few good uses for anger.

◆

When we believe the world is orderly and manageable, we experience anger far more often than is necessary—to our detriment.

Give up some degree of hope. Accept some degree of helplessness. Embrace more chaos and uncertainty. And the old foe anger will show his face less often.

◆

We can spend a lifetime trying to kill, silence, or correct what makes us angry, only to die enraged amidst a world unconquered.

Conquer your anger, and you vanquish all your enemies in one sweep.

◆

The unresolvable chaos of life, which drives our need for order and certainty—and our hostility toward those who seem to oppose or obstruct our sense of order—is the same chaos that should reduce our anger toward others.

◆

In recognizing that we all suffer from the adversity of existence, we can counter anger with compassion and sympathy—for others and for ourselves. When one experiences compassion, anger fades; for while anger seeks to repay suffering, compassion acknowledges it, accepts it, and pities it.

Compassion for suffering is the antidote to anger.

on the self

He himself *is something of an illusion.*

He is not his perceptions. He is not his experiences. He is not his thoughts, decisions, or actions. He is the sum of these parts—everything he experiences and everything he thinks and does in a continual, fluctuating feedback loop. He resides within this loop of the external and internal, the self and other. He is the loop. He is the center—an observer of his consciousness, observing everything.

Inside each of us is something that none of us knows. It is something that takes the raw material of the world and our bodies and produces what we do and who we are—all our thoughts, feelings, and desires. We don't know or control ourselves nearly as well as we'd like to think—perhaps not at all in the way we think.

◆

Examining and learning about yourself and the world rarely leads to enlightenment; more often, it results in alienation, confusion, and despair.

◆

It's okay not to know yourself. No one really does.

◆

We construct our sense of self through the stories we tell ourselves—the narratives we create by threading together moments, each one like a photograph. But we are never just one of these photographs. Like a time-lapse of a landscape, each frame is still; the sense of motion—of story—only arises when the frames are arranged in sequence. This is how the self emerges. In each moment, there is no self. Across time, however, through the sequencing action of memory, we create one.

◆

Without memories, we are merely a locus of experience. With memories, we are a self.

◆

When brain cells die and areas of the brain shrink because of ailments like dementia, where does the self go? Where was it to begin with? At what point, if any, does the death of one's neurons result in the death of one's self?

◆

We are passengers within the system of our being, confined to the flesh and bones of a brittle machine directed by a clump of gelatinous fat inside its head. Our identities are fragile constructions formed from and within this clump, sustained by the imprecise structure of memories—synaptic connections vulnerable to being ripped apart.

◆

The self sits at the intersection of being and nonbeing, creation and negation.

◆

As the world constantly changes, so does the self. Because of this constant change, there is no moment in which an individual can definitively say, "This, now, is me."

◆

Our ego acts as the director and editor of our stories, striving to maintain logical consistency and mass salability to the external world. What an arduous role it bears!

◆

None of us truly knows what it is like to be *us*. We don't know who we are. There is no way to define or make claim to it.

◆

We are conglomerates of otherness. We are landscapes shaped repeatedly by other people and things—architects working from blueprints we never had the chance to check or approve.

◆

We are the products of our experiences and genetics blended together, each gene and each moment dissolving like solutes into the single solution of our being.

◆

What resides in our unconscious mind is, by its very nature, beyond our awareness and control. In almost all cases, it is not caused or managed by us, yet it *is* us. Our unconscious mind determines so much of who we are and what we do.

◆

The mind is in the body, and the body is in the environment. Everything is interdependent and interlocked.

Our self-awareness emerges through it all—at the intersection of mind, body, and environment—constantly altered, never clear or solitary. It is born out of chaos, and thus it is chaos.

◆

The self is not a central entity but a process—a fragile, temporary skin that continually sheds and changes its color.

◆

There is no *authentic self* as many like to claim. How can we authentically be ourselves if we don't know who we are or where we come from? How can we be ourselves if the self is chaotic and constantly changing?

Authenticity is often conflated with consistency and rigidity. But how can anything be both authentic and stable?

◆

Being authentic means not identifying with any singular, fixed self. We can and must be both indefinite *and* authentic. As we move through moments, experiences, and perceptions, our self constantly varies. The malleable, obscure self *is the authentic self.*

◆

To embrace the true nature of the self is to dissolve the concept of the self.

◆

Being yourself and losing yourself are one and the same.

Becoming your present self involves becoming less of your past self.

We must become ourselves constantly and lose ourselves just as often.

◆

Every person is as many people as the moments they live through.

◆

Just as our hair grows a little every day but looks different only every few months, the self is always changing, becoming a version we don't yet know. We only notice the differences upon reflection, once sufficient time has passed.

◆

When we try to figure out *who* we are, we find nothing. We find something only when we look for *what* we are.

◆

The self is the sum of experiences over time. As long as interactions occur among one's brain, body, and environment, one's self is in constant flux. Thus, only when one ceases experiencing anything can it be defined with finality. In this sense, the total, true self only emerges after we are gone. We can never truly know or identify with it. Our total, true self is a parting gift we can never open.

But perhaps a full and good life is one in which we neither need nor care to open this parting gift. Instead, we recognize the constant fluctuation of the self as what we should identify with—the *self* of the *not-self.* We are the whole process, from dust to dust, born, fluttering in the wind, and passing. "A complete life," wrote the American art historian Bernard Berenson, "may be one ending in so full an identification with the not-self that there is no self to die."

on others

He worries about whether people like him, and he does everything he can to ensure that everyone does. He goes certain ways and does certain things. He thinks carefully about what he will say before he says it. Then, he thinks carefully about what he has said after he said it, hopeful he said the right thing to please, endear, entertain, or humor. He cares so much about how he is experienced in the minds of everyone else that he never experiences himself in his own.

It is a strange paradox of narcissism and self-abandonment. He is so desperate, so misguided, and so focused on being liked and seen a certain way that he changes and reduces who he is at every turn.

In the end, he isn't really seen by anyone at all.

We objectify other people, rendering them objects of our perception. In doing this, deep down, we realize that we are also the objects of others' perception.

◆

We only exist insofar as we can construct and define ourselves in relation to others. We are as much others as we are ourselves.

Each of us is a collection of others.

◆

Being strange, irrational, annoying, and difficult are not exceptions to the norm of the human condition; they are the human condition.

◆

To have had a roommate, close friend, sibling, parent, or romantic partner is to know how difficult it is to live with anyone. In their deepest, truest form, everyone is some amount of *unlikable.*

◆

Odds arc, you are far more irritating and flawed than you think—and you probably already think you are very irritating and flawed.

You know there are flaws in you, and you have some idea of what they are. But you don't know what they're really like from the outside—or how bad they really might be. You'll never know.

If you're lucky, someone at some point will become so frustrated by you that they'll hurl all your faults at you in a moment of anger. But even then, you won't fully understand.

◆

One of the most significant things we can learn from getting to know someone *well* is just how little we know anyone at all.

◆

We are always the sole narrator and subject of every story we tell—of every experience we have and every person we know and meet. Because of this, we will always inflate our own importance and miss the truth.

◆

The truth is that the world doesn't see much of us. And it doesn't care much about us. The exception *might* be a few close friends, family members, and romantic partners who do care about us—if we're lucky. But even then, those individuals won't really see much of *us,* either—and the degree to which they care about us is limited and variable. Ultimately, very few people will ever know or care about us in the ways we might think—the ways we project onto others based on our own knowledge and care of ourselves. The downside of all this is that the world doesn't care much about us. The upside is that the world doesn't care much about us. Our mistakes, oversights, and failures will all be forgotten at worst and, more than likely, be missed altogether. The solace to be found in this fact is perhaps worth its bitterness.

◆

The sound of a crowded restaurant, where the music is low and all you can hear is that droning hum of indiscernible chatter—*that* is the sound of the world en masse. We can squawk all we want, but we must understand that most settings are not a theater, but a large eatery filled with other speakers who aren't listening and don't care to. Even if they tried, they wouldn't hear you.

◆

The very existence and popularity of art is a testament to the profound loneliness of humanity.

◆

In our relentless effort to make people like us, to avoid confrontation or causing displeasure, we often end up deceiving others and wasting their time.

Inevitably, we cause the problems we sought to avoid.

◆

If our niceness translates into a sort of passivity, and if we make this sort of niceness our primary goal, we end up concealing our real interests, desires, sensibilities, beliefs, and boundaries.This leads to otherwise good people treating us poorly and inaccurately, inadvertently taking advantage of us. And we become resentful of these people—people who are merely doing their best with the information they have. We are the problem, however. And our misguided niceness is our problem.

◆

To constantly agree with what another person says or wants is not to demonstrate care or respect for them, but rather, to reveal that we care chiefly about how that other person thinks and feels about *us*. This sacrifices an authentic and caring interaction for the sake of self-preservation. The *nice person* is not truly listening or responding to what is being said, done, or requested. They are performing a show for an audience they so desperately want to impress, but with little regard for the actual consequences or outcomes of their performance. They see the audience not as a group of individuals, but as an extension of themselves.

◆

True kindness is distinct from niceness. It isn't always comfortable or easy, and it doesn't always make you the hero, the best person in the room, or the easiest to get along with. Rather, true kindness is challenging. It embraces the pains of honest self-awareness and accepts our meagerness and fallibility; it requires difficult moments, difficult conversations, and difficult positions. True kindness fosters what we hope for in the world: clarity of expectations, authenticity, and genuine respect for others' time and interest.

◆

We fear rejection so much that we never let the world truly know us. In many cases, we never come to truly know *ourselves*. We deny ourselves first, avoiding judgment and rejection by never being ourselves to begin with.

◆

We talk back and forth, anxiously sharing thoughts and ideas in the hope of impressing others. But in prioritizing the comfort of approval, we often subjugate what's honest. We protect ourselves but lose each other. No one really knows anyone.

◆

We worry that we will never find the right person or create the right life, and in doing so, we sacrifice good people and a good life.

◆

There are no right people or right things for anyone.

Finding connections with a few people and developing an affinity for a few things, even if these connections and affinities don't last forever, is likely the best anyone can hope for. The more we run around searching for better people and circumstances, the more we miss out on what is likely *good enough* right now.

◆

"Good enough" is neither insult nor compromise. Life is a struggle filled with uncertainty. History is a record of failure at best and a pit of bloodshed at worst. To find what or who is "good enough" is a wonder that defies the odds of history and warrants the joy of salvation.

on goodness

He fears not only the world outside himself but also the world within. He knows what's outside is always inside. His windows are cracked, and his walls have holes.

Born out of and into the disorder, malice, and destruction of the world, his flesh and mind are woven from the same chaos that forms his environment.

He now finds himself both surrounded by and composed of disorder.

All beings come to exist and operate through the same natural process—a cycle of push and pull, conflict and resolution, growth and destruction, life and death, overcoming and being overcome. Humanity is not exempt from this. We are merely another stop on the train of evolution, fueled by the burning coal of existence, leaving only smoke and debris in its wake. To overcome this reality, we must first acknowledge and accept that we are part of a malignantly destructive process.

Each new passenger and each new train car is an opportunity to alter and improve the train's mechanics, to transcend its current condition. Humanity's unique opportunity for this lies in its self-awareness. At the very least, we can strive to convert the train to electric or solar power.

◆

We want to be good. This desire suggests that we are not inherently good—not entirely, at least. The very aspiration to be good implies that it is not our instinctive state.

There is an inherent duality in our moral nature that necessitates a conscious effort to lean toward goodness. We are both the force fighting against ourselves and the self being fought. We are not solely the good, noble lens through which we discern and apply moral guidance; we are also the flawed and nebulous mechanisms beneath that require such instruction.

◆

We are always on the brink of some form of malevolence, and if we don't pay close attention, we will slip.

◆

The traits and desires we repress are still part of us, influencing our behavior. They dwell and fester in the unconscious, growing stronger over time, striking without our awareness.

◆

The more we repress our malignant qualities, and the more we refuse to acknowledge the duality of good and evil at the core of our being, we risk these qualities becoming unknown to us or, worse, disguised as goodness. We risk growing increasingly wicked; we risk losing sight of what is good.

◆

To improve ourselves, we must be willing to acknowledge the totality of who we are—including our darker qualities (or the potential for them within us).

In the same way we cannot fix a problem we aren't aware of or cure a physical ailment that hasn't been diagnosed, we cannot manage our potential for malice if we do not recognize it exists. Liberation from our negative and harmful qualities does not come from attempting to escape them but from acknowledging and, in some respects, embracing them.

◆

Understanding and accepting ourselves as we really are, the good and the bad, allows us to more easily accept others as they really are. Put differently, recognizing our potential for malice and destruction enables us to exhibit goodness more readily. It allows us to see that we're not so different from others, that even our enemies are much like us.

If, instead, we believe ourselves to be an exception, then the world from our perspective is filled with enemies. We become our own enemy.

To deny that we, too, are part of a nature that carries both ignorance and nobility, both evil and goodness, is to become susceptible to our lesser sides.

◆

Admitting that one is sick is an act of healing.

◆

Nearly every battle, every scapegoat, and every human atrocity stems from ignorance of one's own potential for malice.

◆

We often assume that evil and wrongdoing are *out there* in the world, but never *in* us. This allows evil to reside in us even more potently and dangerously.

◆

Evil arises not only from intentional wrongdoing but often from misguided attempts to do good.

◆

Avoiding self-reflection is a form of paranoia. It's a fearful distrust and suspicion that the things we know about ourselves but won't admit *are true.* And if they are true, then we are not who we think we are or who we hope to be. But let this be clear: No one is who they think they are or who they hope to be.

◆

The more fearful one is, the more dangerous one becomes.

◆

Monsters, too, are tragic victims of themselves.

◆

Recognizing our problems, flaws, and propensity for malice is the first step. However, awareness of our faults does not absolve us of them. We must also work toward being good to be good. This process is never flawless, pure, or in a straight line. We are highly fallible, slippery beings, constantly sliding off course. But if we want to be good, and are actively trying to be good, then we are moving in the right direction.

◆

To feel and know that things can be right or wrong, and to strive to improve and validate this awareness—as individuals and as a species—is to be lucid embodiments of perhaps the most potent and enchanting elixirs the universe has ever created: kindness, love, and hope.

◆

Throughout history, kindness and mutual aid have proven to be the most effective ways for species, communities, and individuals to flourish. For you, for me, for us. True kindness is the cornerstone of all meaningful and fruitful relationships: friendships, romantic partnerships, creative collaborations, family bonds, and the relationships of individuals to society at large. With every gesture of love, every act of generosity, and every demonstration of respect, decency, and moral regard, we have and will continue to survive and thrive.

◆

One of the few things that most modern religions have in common *and* get right is the golden rule, or the *ethic of reciprocity.* Christianity says: "You shall love your neighbor as yourself." Judaism says: "What is hateful to you, do not do to your fellow man." Islam says: "None of you truly believes until he loves for his brother what he loves for himself." Hinduism says: "This is the sum of duty: Do not do to others what would cause pain if done to you." Buddhism says: "Hurt not others in ways that you yourself would find hurtful." Confucianism says: "Do not do unto others what you would not want others to do unto you."

These religions praise different—or no—gods, follow different scriptures, obey different rules, have different orthodoxies, and so on. Yet all of them, using extraordinarily similar language, contain the crux of that golden rule. The near-universal presence of this principle across so many faiths is not proof of its religious origins, but of its centrality to humankind. Kindness is humanity's true religion. It is one of the few genuine gifts of our consciousness—not only the ability to be kind, but the desire to improve and universalize that kindness.

◆

We don't need God or faith to be kind or forgiving or righteous. We simply need to embody these qualities and recognize their obvious value for everything. Even the most selfish individuals, with only a little reflection, will see plainly that the best way to live and to serve oneself is to coexist harmoniously with others—to care, to love, and to be kind.

◆

Humanity paints its self-portrait in every moment and with every act. Each of our lives is a brushstroke in this portrait. It is up to each of us to try to help paint a smile on the face. And it is up to each of us to determine whether that smile is genuine.

◆

If we want a good world, we must believe in a good world. And we must create it based on that belief.

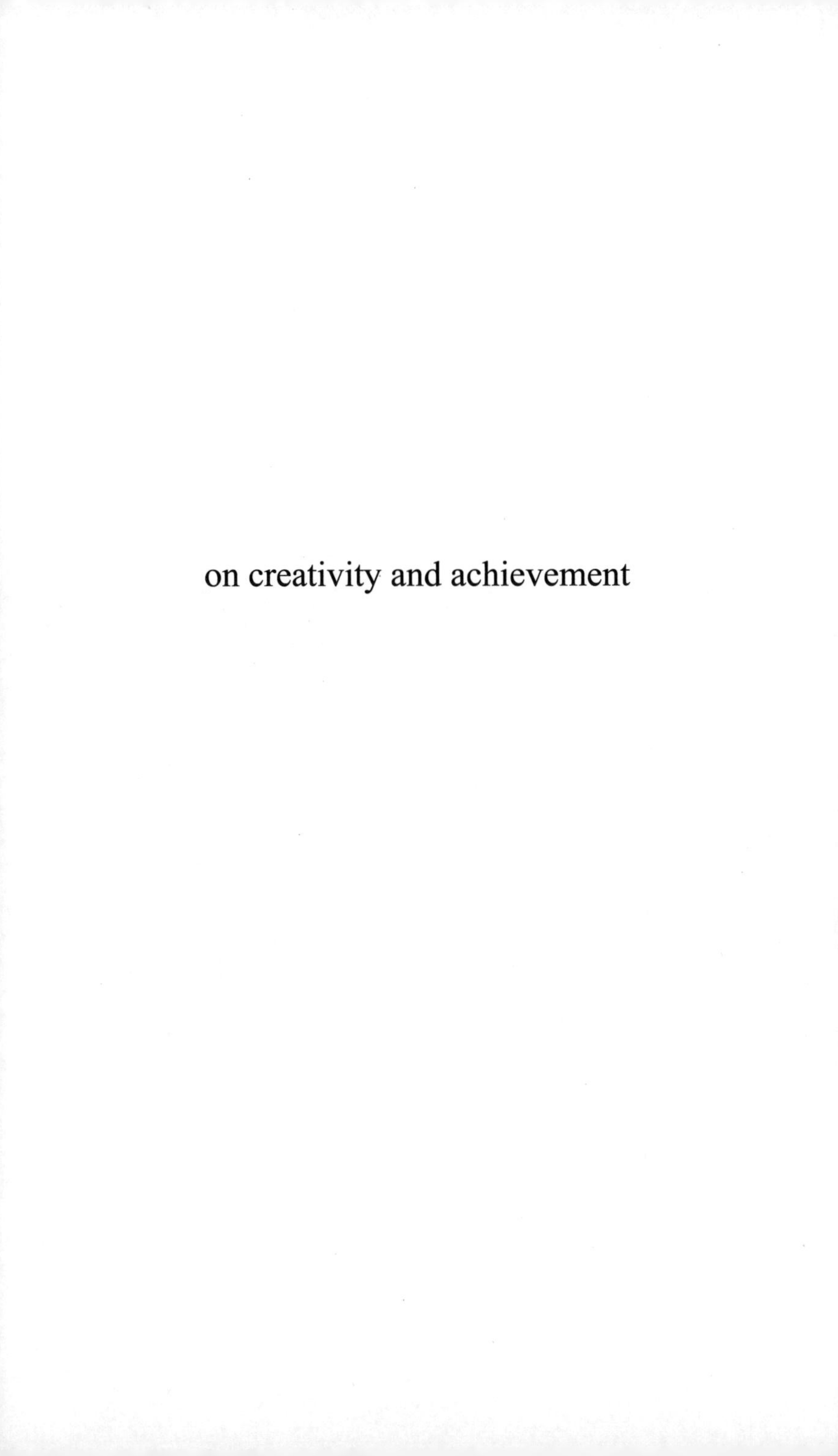

on creativity and achievement

He lays the human psyche bare on the table, dissecting it, so he can see it for what it really is in all its horror. Out oozes the slime of absurdity and the sludge of melancholy—with which he paints; with which he transmutes; through which things become beautiful.

Creativity is both a symptom of self-awareness and its cure.

In medicine, certain preventative and preparative treatments contain forms of the bacteria or virus that causes the disease being treated. Likewise, creativity exposes you to the virus of self-awareness so that you can develop enough immunity to survive it.

The cure is in the ailment.

◆

It is not darkness or depression or anything of the sort that makes art *good*. It is not darkness that is sought after or admired in good art. It is honesty. But if someone is honest, they will inevitably find and reveal notes of darkness, if not complete fear, frustration, angst, dread, depression, and all the other shades of darkness. That is why it is so common for an artist to be *tortured*. Not because being tortured makes good art, but because if you're making good art, how could you not be tortured?

◆

To express and share the dreadful aspects of being is to make the contents of such an expression slightly more bearable.

◆

The admission of hopelessness seems to produce a sort of hope. Somehow, to give up on life can be an act of affirming it. "The fact that life has no meaning is a reason to live—moreover, the only one," wrote Emil Cioran.

To venture into the depths of our being—into the chambers of fear and obscurity—and to speak of them with unwavering honesty is to transmute them into something worth living for; it is to hope.

◆

Even if no one ever really hears you, say it.

◆

Music can explain what reason never will.

◆

One could spend a lifetime describing every detail of a single scene and still never finish.

◆

We are all our own *gods*. Scared. Helpless. Alone at the center of all creation.

◆

We are our only meaning, creating it anew in each new moment, each new discovery, and each new work of art.

◆

Reality uses each of us as its muse, constantly painting and repainting new masterpieces with and through us.

◆

When we create our own meaning, we create our own universe.

Despite accomplishing many things in his life, he often finds himself in the same state as when he started. This is the nature of his condition. After a certain point, achievements no longer satisfy his fundamental yearnings or alleviate his fundamental pains.

Far more unfortunate, however, is that he sometimes finds himself in a worse state than when he began, toiling and struggling only to move further away from his aims, comforts, and orientations. In response to his feeling of lostness and desolation, he is drawn like a moth toward the light of others' homes. He willingly abandons his own goals, his own home, outsourcing his life to others.

His greatest achievement—perhaps his only true achievement—is realizing what achievement means to him and then living accordingly.

So many of us long to be understood, yet we never speak. We yearn for success, yet we never try. We desire *reasonable things,* yet we never ask.

◆

There is nothing to hold out for. As far as anyone knows, there is only one life, and it is this one. Nothing else is guaranteed. What you hold back on while you're here is the only real risk.

◆

Life inevitably involves suffering. It is not about reducing or eliminating suffering but choosing the *objects* for which we suffer.

The task of human existence is to find, live for, and relish, as often as possible, something that makes the horrors and suffering of existence worthwhile—not in spite of them, but in the face of them.

◆

The very process of moving forward toward new circumstances and new selves combats the despair that can arise from a stagnant sense of existence—a sense of directionlessness or inactivity in one's life and self-identity.

We will never reach our true selves or ideal conditions of life, but the continuous movement forward can be enough to satisfy the yearning.

◆

To live is to die. To live well is to have something you fear and dread losing in death. To die well is to have lived well with these things despite the dread and fear.

◆

Generally, most people don't believe in anyone's potential until it's already been realized. And the longer someone tries to realize their potential without success, the less believable it becomes. But success, like all things, unfolds differently and at a different pace for each of us. The only thing that guarantees we'll never achieve something meaningful is no longer trying to achieve it. Otherwise, everything is on the table. All is possible. Ask Nietzsche! Ask Dickinson! Ask van Gogh! Ask Bukowski! Countless people discovered success only in the final act of their lives. Many have lived and died never knowing their potential for success, never knowing how great and capable they were, only to be revered all over the world after their death. Far more have lived and given up, never knowing that success was in the cards—if only they hadn't folded.

◆

The best and most talented individuals in their fields don't achieve success by merit alone. There are innumerable unknowable and often counterintuitive factors that bring people to or keep people from their potential. No one, not even oneself, can ever properly account for or understand their success or the lack thereof.

◆

Sometimes what appears to be misfortune is the very thing that ultimately allows you to discover your strengths and find success. Other times, what appears to be a great stroke of luck is what prevents you from this discovery.

One never knows what is truly good or bad news until everything is over, the curtains shut, and the lights go out.

◆

Don't pretend to know what is coming or when it will arrive. No one knows anything for certain. Keep going. What else is there to do? Life is hell. Light it on fire with the same fervor as the flames that engulf you.

◆

In the end, no one will know or care about you. No one will know or care about anyone. All will be lost to dust and time. The memory of the stars does not contain us. This moment is yours, and yours alone, only once forever. Spend it how you want to—as best you can. And if you don't, don't worry. It's an impossible task—to make the most of moments. But the point is to try.

◆

The most a moment has is what you can give to it.

◆

Ultimately, there is no real audience in the theater of our lives. We have our friends, family, and perhaps—for a few of us—our fans. But they are more like characters in the play than an audience.

We are the only ones truly present in our personal theater. We are simultaneously the director, actor, and the sole individual in the crowd.

We should try to make it a show we don't mind sitting through for several decades.

◆

We often view people with decorated careers, active social lives, busy schedules, and wide-ranging travels as *successful.* But if we could see these individuals in private, or from within their own heads, we might find them lamenting about how stressed, tired, and anxious they are, and how little time they have for themselves and the things they actually want to do. What kind of success is that?

Success is living a life in which the maximum amount of time is spent on the most interesting, enjoyable, fulfilling, and preferred activities, whatever they might be for the individual. How many of the so-called successful people of the world are successful by this metric?

What we want is time spent on things that matter to us. It all boils down to that. The rest is garnish and display. And if only *you* eat the meal of your life, who then is the garnish and display even for?

When you see success in this way—or perhaps when you imagine what it might look like for you in the future—you may find that it's already around you, right within reach.

◆

An exciting life is one in which we are excited to be alive. It is not necessarily one in which we are always frantically doing things.

◆

Life is not lived in the realm of idealization and romanticism. It is lived in the trenches of the day-to-day and the ordinary. And so, that is where we must find and create a comfortable home.

◆

In a world where everyone dies, in a universe where everything ends, those who live quiet, modest, simple lives are just as successful as those who live prominent, active, and demanding ones.

In the end, doing something and doing nothing are the same. The universe consumes everything without regard for taste. No one does anything more or less significant in any grand, objective sense. The only thing that matters is how something feels to the person doing it.

◆

If you want to do something important, decide what is important to you.

◆

When one lives with a deep awareness of the meaninglessness, temporariness, and futility woven into everything, one realizes that their efforts should not be directed toward some endgame, but rather, toward the understanding that there are no endgames. The primary goal is to explore, share, and connect with our present being as honestly and deeply as possible, transmuting the nothing into everything while we can.

◆

People often say that life is lived outside your comfort zone. But what kind of life is always outside comfort? Comfort has somehow become something to avoid or disdain, something to run from. Why? Life is so uncomfortable as it is.

There is, of course, nothing wrong with pushing one's limits, trying new things, facing one's fears, and so on. But there is also nothing wrong with finding and embracing comfort. Being comfortable doesn't mean idleness or complacency. It can simply mean living in a way that feels reasonably secure, content, and focused on what matters and brings joy.

For a busy, type-A kind of person, discomfort might offer a strange sort of comfort. And that's fine. But even in this, discomfort is really just another form of comfort. What we always prefer is comfort, however that looks for us.

◆

The *fear of missing out* tends to focus on what others are doing—that we aren't. But truly missing out happens when we follow others at the expense of our own interests. This is how we miss out on our own lives.

◆

Perhaps out of all the things we want, simplicity and calmness are the closest we can get to bringing an end to wanting itself.

◆

The world doesn't owe us anything, and we don't owe the world anything, either.

◆

There is no greater success than staying sane, compassionate, focused, and self-honest. However we are able to do this, we ought to.

That is hard enough. That is successful enough.

on regret

He constantly desires something better, something other than what he has chosen and ended up with. He is tormented by an unending barrage of what-ifs. *But he will never know how things might or could have been. All he has is the certainty of what is.*

It is incredibly overwhelming to choose anything. To move forward in one direction is to eliminate the possibility of every other direction. *But what if the other directions are better?* We might wonder. We'll never know. We can never know. And it doesn't matter. Life being *better* has nothing to do with the other directions we theoretically could have gone. No matter what path we choose in life, there will always be things worth regretting if we see regret as a sensible response to life. There will always be people, events, and circumstances to dread and loathe. Much of life is dreadful. But that is true regardless of the way we go or don't go. Living a better life does not depend on having chosen a better direction, but on seeing *this direction,* the only direction, better.

◆

We are given the steering wheel of a vehicle moving at full speed. No brakes. No navigation system. Occasionally, we turn in the *right* direction. Most turns, however, send us in unforeseen and unknown directions.

Our hope must be to make the most of where we end up, not to end up where we wanted.

◆

There is no pause button on life; no fast forward; no rewind. There is only one continuous sequence of *now*. The film reel is always spinning. The frames are always passing by the projector's lamp. Every frame must be watched. And we must choose how we watch it—what we pay attention to and how we interpret what we see. This is all we can do. Watch. And watch wisely. Enjoy the film—the conflict and resolution, the good and the bad.

◆

We are aware of our unawareness. We know we don't know how things will go tomorrow, let alone ten years down the line. And yet we regret things constantly.

Regret is an absurd conscious response to the inabilities of consciousness. It is the refusal of consciousness to accept its limits. *I can imagine the future, I can worry about the future, and I can plan for the future. Why then can't I control the future?!* consciousness wonders.

Regret occurs when the paradox of self-awareness—the fact that we are aware of so much but given control of nothing—is never acknowledged as paradoxical. If we recognize the true scope of our unawareness and the limits of our control, it becomes obvious that we never have anything to regret.

◆

Regret is a cognitive bias.

◆

It is the curse of nostalgia to look back on the past and see only the highlight reel and none of the pain.

◆

There is nothing we can love without also, at times, strongly disliking it.

◆

If we regret and loathe our life, it is likely not our life that is the problem, but our expectations of it.

◆

Expectations are life's worst contaminant.

◆

You've ruined so many moments. Try not to ruin more moments fretting about the ones you've already ruined.

You cannot change the moments you've ruined, but you can change how you view those moments moving forward.

◆

If you don't get upset at yourself for being unhappy, you might be a little happier some of the time.

◆

We can only do what we've done, and we could only have done what we did. If we were to go back to a moment in the past as ourselves, when faced with a decision in that moment again, we might imagine we could choose differently than we had. But, as our past selves, we would undoubtedly make the same decision our past selves already made. Again. And again. And again. How could we do otherwise? We can never escape the conditions of that moment: the information we possessed, the scope of our foresight and awareness, our mood and feeling, our exposure to recent influences. Those factors create the same equation with the same output every time. Two plus two is always four.

◆

It is the nature of consciousness to see how everything goes and to plead and cry for it to be different. But it won't be different. It can't be different.

◆

If, in the past, we couldn't know where our decisions would lead, couldn't predict what was going to happen in the world more broadly, why would we now assume we can know and predict these things? Why would we think we can do or redo anything better than we did? There are infinite potential paths in life. Knowledge of how this one has gone does not improve our understanding of any other; it doesn't reveal to us how any other path would've turned out.

◆

The only way to ensure one does not regret and loathe their life is to love and embrace it.

◆

To loathe, to regret, and to desire to change what has happened in one's life is to resent life itself. Life is always and only how it goes. To wish it went differently is to wish away life itself.

◆

How can we expect anything good to come if we refuse to enjoy what is good now?

◆

To live a day fully is to live in the moment. But there are many days to be lived, and to live a day fully risks losing or harming the other days. To regret a day fully is to think you can somehow reconcile this dichotomy.

◆

In the end, it is not the specific decisions we make that give our lives meaning; it is how we consider and view the life our decisions have led us to.

◆

If you want to enjoy life more, you can. Life doesn't have to change. *You* can.

◆

Regret is a prison in which the prisoners are also the guards.

on hope

It's the greatest show ever, and he has a front row seat.

He exists in a brain that creates and finds meaning in its unique experience of everything—a brain that wants and cares and tries. Though he may be deeply limited and unaware, he is still the experiencer of it all. He can still find beauty in it. The illusion is real; the illusion is wonderous; the illusion is worth it.

He sees it all flailing so violently and yet so perfectly.

Despite humanity's great conflicts, it has, in many remarkable ways, come together. Though deeply challenged and imperfect, we have forged ahead and created a world for ourselves.

We have built roads and buildings and cities; we have preserved wonders of nature and small towns from history; we have devised systems to manage global conditions and functions; we have produced arts and cultures and ways to share what otherwise could never be known or perceived; we have developed technologies that make the impossible possible, right in the palm of one's hand; we have invented reasons for it all. And all this has been accomplished with nothing but the raw materials of the Earth and our minds.

◆

Humanity's most absurd and most beautiful quality is its ability to find enough reason to continue—a string of life always extending outward, reaching with excitement and wonder into the impossibility of everything.

◆

To not only endure the suffering of existence but also to facilitate and preserve it with such fervor is a testament to both humanity's unfathomable strength and unfathomable ignorance. We are unwaveringly powerful, undeniably impressive, ridiculously foolish, absurdly masochistic, and unquestionably beautiful.

◆

To perceive something so blatantly ugly and horrific, yet to cry at the beauty you find in it—that is the task of human existence.

◆

Sometimes, the only way to experience the beauty of things is to think about things in a beautiful way.

◆

Hope is an otherwise impossible ideal, made possible only by the relentless perseverance of a humanity that, time and time again, refuses to fold in the game of existence.

◆

The true leap of faith in life is not in believing that some meaning or point exists beyond you or this life. There is likely nothing to hope for or believe in after your final breath, and nothing beyond your comprehension and experience. The only seemingly reasonable and worthwhile leap of faith, then, is in believing that what exists down here on the ground, right now, in front of and around you—what you can know and experience—is enough.

◆

Perhaps salvation is not found through reason or resolution, but through the liberation of the need for either. We seek not a resolution but the ability to act and sustain without one. That is true hope.

◆

Perhaps our problem lies not in our lack of answers, but in asking the wrong questions.

Why are we here? Where are we going? Where did we come from? No. Ask instead: *How do we make the most of being anywhere without having any apparent reason to be somewhere?*

◆

Just as a chisel, pen, or pot is man-made and used solely by and for humanity, yet each remains *real* and usable, so too might be the case for meaning. Meaning is man-made, subjective, and without use or merit beyond humanity, yet it remains a profound expression of human ingenuity and an undeniably useful tool for human experience.

◆

Meaning is an illusion; everything is an illusion. But realizing this doesn't mean we suddenly understand how the illusions work or stop experiencing their apparent magic. Illusions are illusions because they work. Knowing that meaning, free will, and the self are illusions does not diminish their profound illusory nature. The tricks of meaning, free will, selfhood, and existence are still performed beautifully, and we are still enthralled.

◆

It's all insane; everything is absurd. But the fact that humanity has created any semblance of goodness out of it all is as miraculous as existence itself.

◆

Miracles are real, and they are created by the hands and minds of the godlike force of humanity.

◆

Surely humanity will go on to discover new realms of the cosmos, unlock new laws of physics, and develop new technologies, but perhaps its greatest achievement will be the development of a new philosophy, science, or some combination thereof that provides a robust way of thinking about the meaning of life—without compromise, blind faith, or pure imagination.

At some point in human history, philosophies like nihilism, rationalism, empiricism, relativism, existentialism, absurdism, Taoism, Buddhism, and Stoicism did not exist. The same goes for every branch of science. Since the onset of consciousness and self-awareness, since the first questions were asked, we have been pulling worms out of the philosophical can. Surely, there are more worms still in there. And perhaps, at some point in the future, we will find something different, something reconciliatory—if nothing else, the shelter of a giant, empty can.

◆

Life is but a series of new views from new places, both individually and collectively. Unity, purpose, and the reason to continue are found in a shared desire for the new, the novel, and the wondrous. There is an infinity out there waiting. We want to see it. We want to touch it. We will suffer for the hope of it.

◆

In the face of inevitable loss and ultimate meaninglessness, it can be terrifying to assert that things are profound and beautiful, and it can seem absurd to imbue life with any personal meaning. On the other side of any moment, it could all be taken away from you—from all of us. Yet it is impossible to live as a conscious being without finding things to be profound, beautiful, and meaningful. We are inescapably compelled to fall in love with so many aspects of life, whether we think it wise or not, absurd or not.

◆

Finding existence beautiful and worthwhile is like smiling through a beating. What's scarier and more intimidating than someone who smiles while being beaten?

We have the endurance and resilience of a species that has been abused by everything, including itself, yet has sustained not only its existence but also its hope and desire for existence. We have taken the dysfunctions and paradoxes of our being and, through our self-awareness, learned how to endure, transmute, and, with the right effort, love them all.

In us, the universe meets its match. It *will* win. But we will undoubtedly put up the best fight it's seen yet.

◆

If you want to love life, love this right now.

◆

As long as you're alive, there is hope.

on free will

Everything he does, he does either because he wants to or because he has to. He doesn't choose when he has to do something, and he has no control over what he wants.

He is not the driving force of his life; he is the subject of it. He is the product of an endless web of other forces and circumstances, of which he is barely aware, let alone directing.

We tend to think that what is outside us is largely beyond our control, while what is inside our minds is within our control. But in terms of control, there is no real difference between the internal and external realms. They are two sides of the same coin.

We do not decide what makes us scared or what makes us feel good. We do not control how our mind and body react to these things. We do not fundamentally control the mechanisms of our body and brain. At our core, we are just as out of control of ourselves as we are of the world.

◆

Freedom is a non sequitur of existence. No being ultimately controls themselves any more than they control the wind. We are not merely dust in the wind; we are one and the same with it.

◆

No one chose their first thoughts.

No one chooses their next thoughts.

◆

We exist within a constantly fluctuating structure—our physical, cognitive, and environmental condition—always unsure of what we might do next.

◆

Our decisions began long before we could make them.

We were all created by a series of decisions that began before we even understood what a decision was, before we even existed, before anyone existed—and now, to keep this whole process going, we are continually forced to make more decisions.

◆

Our lack of freedom is made blatantly apparent by our desires. If we truly possessed free will, would we have any *undesirable* desires? Wouldn't we all live perfect lives and have perfect habits and interests? Wouldn't we choose to exclusively desire healthy routines, meaningful work, and socially valuable things? Wouldn't we choose to desire habits and traits that allow us to obtain these things?

It's often said that some people have less willpower than others. But willpower doesn't occur in degrees. One either has it or does not. One is either free to determine their desires or they are not. And the fact that everyone knows certain things are better for them, but only some individuals engage in those things, is proof not of any variance in willpower but of a lack of freedom over the will. Individuals who form and reshape their habits toward more *desirable* things over time must possess a desire to form or reshape their desires, which is itself a desire. Did these individuals choose this desire and ability any more than those who did not? To what can the better-off individual attribute their desire? Perhaps the desire to be healthier and better off. But to what can they attribute *that* desire? Perhaps the desire to live longer, feel better, make more money, or look better. But to what can they attribute *that* desire? Biological or sociological influences?

Ah, sweet freedom! In the words of Arthur Schopenhauer: "Man can do what he wills, but he cannot will what he wills."

◆

We are not the drivers of ourselves. If we are lucky, our autonomous vehicle encounters the right input data and receives the latest software updates more often than the average. That's the best we can hope for.

◆

The only thing more powerful within the human condition than the desire for complete freedom is the impossibility of attaining such a state.

◆

At the top of the pyramid of human freedoms—where an individual has attained physical freedom (the ability to move around unrestrictedly), political freedom (the ability to think, speak, and act without constraint beyond moral and legal parameters), and financial freedom (the ability to sufficiently provide for oneself)—the individual still remains deeply unfree, confined within a body, a mind, and a natural world. They are told what to do, when to do it, and why *by themselves*.

◆

Humanity seeks to be free, working to create a world that mirrors its vision of freedom, striving to unfasten the shackles of the forces that impose on it, only to be left, if it can even achieve this much, still desiring freedom from itself.

◆

There is no more absurd image than an individual claiming to be a freethinker in a mind and world they did not choose and cannot control.

There are no freethinkers. Even the most so-called original freethinkers are not free; they have simply been compelled to deviate from the norm. *Compelled*—the antithesis of freedom. These individuals are valuable members of the world, yes, but they are not free from it.

◆

The self-made person must have made themselves out of nothing.

◆

In a world of infinite possibilities, to do whatever one chooses whenever one chooses without restraint or imposition, without any force guiding oneself, would perhaps be the true prison.

◆

The goal is not to be completely free but to be free from the very conception of freedom. "You can only be free," wrote Gibran, "when even the desire of seeking freedom becomes a harness to you, and when you cease to speak of freedom as a goal and a fulfillment."

◆

The free person is perhaps merely conscious of the necessity of all things, including their own lack of freedom.

◆

The intellectual resistance to the likely fact that humanity has no free will—as most of us define it—is understandable. At first glance, this fact appears to deprive life of its already difficult, minute meaning. If we are our last hope of creating meaning in the void of the cosmos, the last line of defense against the nothingness and futility of all things, then what are we left with if we are not even in control of ourselves? While there may seem to be a contradiction between believing there is no free will and continuing to make decisions and forge meaning for ourselves, there isn't.

In truth, to say that life is meaningless because we have no say in its unfolding is, once again, to succumb to our lack of free will. We did not choose to decide that life is meaningless, so why should this declaration hold any more weight than its opposite—that life is still meaningful? Ultimately, a being does not choose to create meaning or not. They simply create it or they don't. And as humans, *we* do.

Meaning is found and experienced by virtue of one's unique experience of life. This does not change with or without free will. If we are passengers on a train or in a car—even if we have no control over where we are going, why, or how—our view of the passing landscape touches our heart just the same. It is no less beautiful. Our mind's interpretation is no less valuable and meaningful to us.

Even if we know free will does not exist, we cannot live any other way than we already do. We must carry on as we do, and we must care as much as we do. Free will is not only an illusion; it is an inescapable one.

on everything

Whether he wants it or not, no matter what he does, he has been and will always be a part of everything. His existence was written into the script of the cosmos. And now, what he writes, however seemingly insignificant, continues to affect the story forever—even after he is gone.

No one is steering this world's movement. Each of us is dealt a different, complex, nuanced hand of good and bad luck, which we can neither understand nor control, and which shapes who we are and aren't. To exempt anyone from this implies that everyone and everything is exempt. To put anyone at fault puts everyone and everything at fault.

◆

The life and death of every species and the existence of every object have been essential to the whole—to this moment, to everyone, to everything. We are all part of the grand design, the great show—whyever, by, and for *whomever* it is made and performed. Every species and every individual are part and parcel of what makes the world what it is and what it will become.

◆

Until you realize the credit or blame for anything is owed to everyone and everything, you will never see the *truth*.

◆

When a microbe kills another microbe, we don't notice. When a random plant is ripped from the ground by a hurricane, we don't care. When a lion eats a wildebeest, we don't question it. We say: *It is the way of nature; it is the way of the animal kingdom.* But when something is done to us, whether by a human, other organism, or natural force, it is always good or bad, triumph or tragedy. To what kingdom do we think we belong? To what castle have we been given the keys?

Of course, we feel good or bad when something happens to us or to those we care about—our family, friends, country, or species. And since we feel good or bad, we make declarations of *goodness* and *badness*. But when we speak of good and bad, we never refer to objective goodness or badness. How could we? We have no idea what's truly good or bad. It's incoherent to even suppose such a possibility. Good for what? Bad for what? There is nothing objective to which to ascribe this qualitative orientation—no external reference point, no objective endgame. Everything is a projection of humanity's anthropocentric view and each person's subjective view within that horizon.

In truth, objectively, everything is either all good or all bad, or nothing is either.

◆

A man walking down a sidewalk stops another man and asks for directions. The man provides the directions, which delays the other man by approximately thirty seconds. On his drive home, this man hits a young girl who runs into an otherwise empty intersection just as he crosses it. The girl is paralyzed.

As a result of her paralysis, throughout her childhood and adolescence, the girl is heavily exposed to various treatments and medical technologies—mobility devices, bionic limbs, and potential brain-machine interfaces. She becomes increasingly enthralled by these technologies, leading her to a career as a biomedical engineer. She excels in this field, and she leads the development of advanced, life-changing prosthetics and brain-machine interface devices for paraplegics, quadriplegics, amputees, and others. However, some of these technologies, particularly her advanced robotics and their capacity to integrate with the human mind, are later used heavily in war, resulting in the deaths of millions.

If it weren't for that little girl and the unsuspecting man delayed by thirty seconds, millions of people who were otherwise murdered might still be alive today.

Of course, this is fiction. And of course, even in this vignette, the man who asked for directions is not responsible for any of what went on to happen. But in at least some limited sense, he participated in causing it.

How would things have gone if he had known where he was going? How would things go if any of us knew where we were going?

◆

Only the inescapable web of cause and effect that we are all trapped within can truly be held responsible for anything.

◆

We can never know the effects of our actions as they span time and space. Thus, we can never know if our existence results in a net positive, net negative, or net neutral effect.

Theoretically, even the most positive-seeming actions could, in varying levels of causation, potentially lead to terrible events in this world. Likewise, something seemingly negative could prevent something far, far worse.

◆

In the end, it is possible that our work—our existence more broadly—causes dangers and problems that we can never imagine and will never know about.

◆

We simply do not and cannot fully comprehend enough about the world—even just our version of it—to know what is truly good or bad.

◆

Life is a continual sequence of gains and losses, ups and downs, pushes and pulls, catastrophes and prosperities. It is only in the myopic view of an individual conscious entity at a single moment in time that something can be considered good or bad.

◆

As long as we continue to believe we know what is ultimately good or bad, we will continue to play God in a reality that does not allow us to play with or as imaginary characters.

◆

We are all part of the incomprehensibly chaotic vehicle of reality, each individual—and each individual's actions—propelling and changing reality's direction.

◆

If determinism is true, you were always part of the universe. From the moment of its conception, you were here—all the particles of your being present and ready for *you*.

You were always going to exist, and there is no version of this universe in which you don't. The universe was created with you in *mind*. You were and are forever trapped in the mystical oneness of all things.

◆

Ultimately, we can never know the ripples in reality we create with each stone's throw. But we *can* know that, in each moment, we stand at the water's edge with access to stones of various sizes. Our tosses send stones skipping across the surface, briefly entertaining us before they submerge beyond sight—yet the stones and their effects go on forever.

◆

No matter what one does in this life, one's actions will reverberate outward, altering everything eternally.

We largely base our self-worth and meaning on our sense of personal significance, often deriving this sense from feeling part of something bigger than ourselves. We yearn for this whether we realize it or not, whether we believe it to be rational or not. This is the desire that drives religion, science, technology, society, and progress. We seek to transcend—to find, create, or believe in a meaning beyond us. But these things ultimately fail us. They are either untrue, incomplete, or unable to provide us with a stable orientation. Religion is illusory, progress is unending, and science and technology appear only to reveal our insignificance. In the end, we are left empty-handed.

But there is one source of true significance that doesn't require any grand illusions, ultimate achievements, or faith in anything.

In every moment, our seemingly insignificant choices and actions can and often do lead to huge changes across time and space. *The butterfly effect.*

Chaos theory, a branch of science and mathematics, shows that, in chaotic systems like reality, even small changes can compound and lead to massive, unpredictable outcomes. And we, of course, are part of this system of reality.

Everything we do in this life will shape the future. Our significance is unbounded; our consolation is chaos.

◆

Perhaps the closest thing to a solution to the conundrum of self-awareness is not a solution at all. Rather, it is a relinquishment of expectation—of all certainty, control, and resolution—and a commitment to simply moving with, observing, and appreciating everything as it is, as deeply and often as possible, while trying our best to be okay. To cry. To love. To try. To fail. To be. To die.

This is hardly a solution in the traditional sense; one can't easily just implement it, dusting off one's hands with a sense of achievement and relief. Despite its almost banal simplicity, perceiving existence with this sort of passive fortitude is extremely difficult. But it's possible—even if only in brief moments.

◆

When we see the whole of nature, we recognize that all things that happen are inevitable and necessary, that what is "good" or "bad" is relative to us, that events are an impersonal unfolding of time and space, that we are no more or less important than anything else, and that everyone and everything became a part of the whole without choosing to be. We are each a single particle amidst an eternal substance in continual motion and reconfiguration. When we see this, when we realize our meekness and our interconnectedness with everything, influenced by an endless chain of causality we can't control, we become less rigidly attached to what has been and will come; we become less anxious about doing exactly the right or wrong thing, less regretful, less scornful—and we become more indifferent to what we cannot change. We understand the storms, the lions, the snakes, the people; and finally, we gain a sense of poise, liberation, and peace.

He is not his conscious mind, and he is not his unconscious mind. He is not his heart, his arms, his legs, his feet, his skin, his face. He is not what is inside him, what's on his surface, or what's outside him. He is nothing on its own.

He is everything passing by the window of his consciousness. He sits in a rare position, in the rarest car on the train of evolution—one with windows. *Through these windows, he observes the material of everything—the very material from which he is made—and he finds beauty in it. He interprets it and creates meaning out of it; he creates the very concept of meaning. He feels pain and confusion and love and hope. He tries and fails. He lives and dies.*

Acknowledgments

Thank you to my agent, Steve Harris, for fervently believing in me and this project—and for going up to bat for it. Thank you to Melissa Zahorsky (and Andrews McMeel Publishing) for seeing and respecting the vision of this book—and for so thoughtfully and carefully helping bring it to life. Thank you to all the readers, listeners, and watchers of my work and of Pursuit of Wonder—you make projects like this possible. And thank you to my parents, friends, and girlfriend for the love, support, and meaning.

Bibliography

Becker, Ernest. *The Denial of Death.* Simon & Schuster: Free Press Paperbacks, 1997.

Berenson, Bernard. *Sketch for a Self-Portrait.* Pantheon Books, 1949.

Camus, Albert. *The Myth of Sisyphus and Other Essays.* Translated by Justin O'Brien. Vintage Books, 1955.

Cioran, E. M. *Anathemas and Admirations.* Translated by Richard Howard. Arcade Publishing, 2012.

Cioran, E. M. *On the Heights of Despair.* Translated by Ilinca Zarifopol-Johnston. University of Chicago Press, 1996.

Dawkins, Richard. *The Selfish Gene.* Oxford University Press, 2016.

Gibran, Kahlil. *The Prophet (Collins Classics).* William Collins, 2020.

Harari, Yuval Noah. *Sapiens: A Brief History of Humankind.* Harper Perennial, 2018.

Harding, Douglas Edison. *On Having No Head.* Shollond Trust, 2013.

Lovecraft, H. P. *The Call of Cthulhu and Other Stories.* Edited by Leslie S. Klinger. Liveright Publishing, 2022.

Sam Harris, host. *The Essential Sam Harris.* Episode 9. "Making Sense of Death." May 26, 2023. https://www.samharris.org.

Nagel, Thomas. "What Is It Like to Be a Bat?" *The Philosophical Review* 83, no. 4 (October 1974): 435–50.

Planck, Max. *Where Is Science Going?* Translated by James Murphy. Inktank Publishing, 2019.

Schopenhauer, Arthur. *On the Freedom of the Will.* Blackwell, 1985.

Thacker, Eugene. *Horror of Philosophy.* Vol. 1, *In the Dust of This Planet.* Zero Books, 2011.

Tom F. Driver. "Beckett by the Madeleine," *Columbia University Forum* 4.3 (1961): 21–25.

Wittgenstein, Ludwig. *Tractatus Logico-Philosophicus.* Translated by Charles Kay Ogden. Benediction Classics, 2019.

About the Author

Robert Pantano is the author of several books, including *The Art of Living a Meaningless Existence, The Art of Living an Absurd Existence,* and *Notes from the End of Everything.* He is also the writer and creator behind the YouTube channel and production house Pursuit of Wonder, where he explores philosophy, science, and literature through short stories, guided experiences, video essays, and more. His work has resonated with millions of viewers and readers around the world. Through it, he strives to contribute to the great human undertaking of finding and creating meaning.